CREATING INDEPENDENT READERS

DEVELOPING WORD RECOGNITION SKILLS IN K–12 CLASSROOMS

Beth Hurst
Cindy Wilson
Deanne Camp
Genny Cramer

SOUTHWEST MISSOURI STATE UNIVERSITY

Holcomb Hathaway, Publishers
Scottsdale, Arizona 85250

Library of Congress Cataloging-in-Publication Data

Creating independent readers : developing word recognition skills in K-12 classrooms /
Beth Hurst ... [et al.].
  p. cm.
  Includes bibliographical references and index.
  ISBN 1-890871-36-2
  1. Word recognition.   I. Hurst, Beth.

LB1050.44.C74 2002
428.4—dc21   2001039110

Copyright © 2002 by Holcomb Hathaway, Publishers, Inc.

Holcomb Hathaway, Publishers, Inc.
6207 North Cattletrack Road
Scottsdale, Arizona 85250
(480) 991-7881
www.hh-pub.com

10 9 8 7 6 5 4 3 2

ISBN 1-890871-36-2

Printed in the United States of America.

CONTENTS

UNIT 1

Word Recognition   1

AN OVERVIEW

UNIT 2

Breaking It Down   13

A LOOK AT MAJOR WORD RECOGNITION SKILLS

Supporting Skills   63

Putting It All Together   83

LIST OF STRATEGIES (ACTIVITIES)

(You may also locate strategies alphabetically by name in the index.)

PREFACE

At no recent time has interest in word recognition, and particularly phonics, been as high as it is currently. Even when Rudolph Flesch wrote *Why Johnnie Can't Read* in 1957, the back-to-basics movement that ensued was of most interest to professionals in the field—teachers, counselors, and principals—whereas the current impassioned concern comes from legislators, parents, and the public. Parents and the American public have expressed a renewed commitment to having children acquire strong word recognition skills. State legislatures are mandating teacher testing for competencies in reading instruction. Perhaps more than ever before, teachers need to be prepared thoroughly with theoretical and research-based knowledge to support effective use of word recognition skills. The intent of this book is to provide future and in-service teachers with an understanding of how to use, teach, and assess the word recognition skills that students need.

In this book, the term *word recognition* is used to describe skills sometimes labeled word identification, word attack, decoding, or similar phrases. Harris and Sipay (1990) state that decoding "involves using a variety of skills, including phonics, to approximate the spoken form of a printed word" (p. 432). We use the term *word recognition* to encompass the ways of determining what a word is, whether sounding it out, using word structure, syllables, context, or other means. When noneducators talk about word recognition, however, they typically use the term *phonics* to represent all word identification skills, or at least phonic analysis and structural analysis. Parents, politicians, and others normally would not know the difference between skills related to the sound–symbol relationship (phonics) and skills related to syllabication, accented syllables, roots, prefixes, and suffixes (structural analysis). Professionals, on the other hand, may take interested nonprofessionals' words literally, assuming that they want only phonics instruction.

Despite this unfortunate confusion, what professionals and nonprofessionals alike want is for students to have all the skills they need to read well. Recognizing this, we have chosen to use the more inclusive term *word recognition* rather than the more restrictive term *phonics* and to address multiple word recognition skills instead of merely phonics. Phonics is just one piece of the puzzle—one tool readers can apply to recognize new words as they gain fluency in reading. By using the broader term *word recognition,* we emphasize the importance of additional skills that can be used to strengthen or improve word identification and understanding.

In helping students become successful users of language, word recognition plays a vital role in both formal and informal ways. Teachers make critical decisions preparing and delivering lessons in word recognition skills based upon their students' needs. The order in which these skills are taught or reinforced may differ as the developmental levels of students emerge in classrooms, whether those learners are the readers of this book or K–12 students. Vygotsky (1978) urges educators to help learners within their zone of proximal development, the potential level at which they can function successfully with help from others. Wishon, Crabtree, and Jones (1998) state that "children seem to learn language in a somewhat intuitive way" (p. 154). As they learn and develop their awareness of language, they subconsciously apply the rules and patterns that govern how to use language. Although children naturally and informally learn many language and word recognition skills, additional formal instruction may have to be provided. Careful monitoring of students' formal and informal use of word recognition skills while reading various texts informs teachers about when to teach specific strategies.

This book is designed to explain word recognition skills and provide practical suggestions for teachers and students. Sections throughout the book provide working definitions for individual word recognition skills, strategies for teaching beginning and experienced readers, strategies that readers can learn to apply during their own reading, and ways to assess how effectively students use their word recognition skills. To help teachers locate and use appropriate activities, we identify strategies as most suitable for primary, intermediate, middle school, secondary, ESL (English as a second language), or all levels.

This book provides information that teachers can use in various instructional contexts with their students, matching student needs and learning styles with instructional practices. For this reason, we have chosen not to address or debate the varying philosophies of teaching reading but instead look at specific word identification skills. No matter what reading philosophy a teacher espouses, teaching word recognition skills is an important, necessary element for teaching reading.

This book is further intended to serve as a resource for teachers to use in supporting their classroom instruction of reading and in understanding the connection between word recognition skills and comprehension. Whether readers are young children learning to read, middle level and high school students developing as readers, or other individuals who are just learning to read or are new to the English language, this text may extend teachers' repertoires of skills and teaching strategies. When teachers have strong background knowledge of word recognition skills, they can better assist students in successfully applying strategies necessary to comprehend texts.

Middle level and secondary teachers in content areas should have a strong foundation in word recognition to support their students' reading of more complex texts. Pikulski (1997–98) states that it is not the responsibility of middle level teachers "to broadly address reading skills or to offer remedial reading instruction; however, since content area texts are such primary vehicles for acquiring subject matter knowledge, teachers must be prepared to help their students effectively comprehend those texts" (p. 36). Consequently, teachers at any grade level and in varying subject areas can benefit from broadening their knowledge of word recognition skills and by understanding the implication of the critical need for students' ability to use such skills throughout life.

A closer look at word recognition skills, how to teach them, various strategies to support the understanding and applications, and methods for assessing students' progress can help classroom teachers help students become better readers. We hope this text will be a valuable tool as teachers go about the important task of helping children become lifelong readers and learners.

ACKNOWLEDGMENTS

When our writing team first gathered almost five years ago, we started with a single objective, which then blossomed into a garden of ideas that we have cultivated carefully during our journey of learning and writing. It seemed the more we talked and wrote, the more we learned. Many of the ideas we wrote about grew out of our new, shared knowledge. When we wrote together, our writing at first conveyed four individual voices, but when merged it became a different, and we hope stronger, voice. We value greatly the lessons we shared along the way that in turn transformed our thinking and teaching.

This book expresses many voices other than those of its authors. It holds the voices of the many people who influenced us during our lives and careers and during the writing process. We gratefully acknowledge some of their contributions below.

First, without the encouragement and belief in us held by Colette Kelly, our editor, we probably would have dropped the ball early on in this process. Her vision sustained us when our hectic schedules seemed to take over our precious time for writing. We thank her and our production director, Gay Pauley, who continued to see the potential for this book from its onset through its completion.

Second, we wish to thank our reviewers, who helped us surpass our original goals for this book. We owe a special thanks to Shirley LeFever-Davis, University of Arkansas, Fayetteville; Becky Huechteman, Evangel University; Leanna Manna, Villa Maria College; and Tom Cornell, Rockwood School District, for their words of encouragement and suggestions on the first draft of the manuscript. They challenged us and confirmed a need for this type of text. They were instrumental in helping us to create a book that is thorough but easy to use. And they inspired us to seek new ideas by reaching out to other teachers, other professionals, leaders in the field, and children and parents.

As we progressed into later drafts of the book, other reviewers assisted us in refining our own thoughts, practices, and writings. Leslie McIlquham, Missouri Reading Initiative, added to the precision of our language and ideas. Jana Loge, Missouri Reading Initiative, in her own uncompromising style, offered helpful and constructive suggestions. Barbara Carnagey, Miller School District, shared outstanding ideas and suggestions, and the input from Laurie Williams, University of Pittsburgh, was extensive, exhaustive, and incredibly valuable in crystallizing our wording. Judy Brunner, Springfield Public Schools, and Toni Briegel, Southwest Missouri State University, shared their expertise and challenged us to fortify the middle and secondary school perspectives because of tremendous need for word recognition skills at this level.

We offer a special thanks to teachers of the past, present, and future for their dedication to helping develop independent readers.

Finally, thank you to our children and grandchildren, for showing us how it works, and our family and friends, for their patience and understanding.

To the
STUDENT

Why do you need a book about word recognition? Because it has become more critical that every teacher have knowledge about how readers figure out words and word meanings as they come in contact with various texts. Suppose you were asked what you know about word recognition. You might respond, "I don't know anything about phonics" or "I don't know anything about word recognition skills." And yet, if you are able to read this text, you do know about word recognition skills and you are applying them right now.

When you come to a new word, do you ever sound it out to see if you recognize it once you have heard it? Do you ever look at the word and see if you recognize any parts of it, such as the prefix or suffix, or perhaps you know the root or base word? What about using the rest of the words in the sentence to see if you can figure it out that way? Or do you use clues such as determining which part of speech the word would be by using your knowledge of language? If so, you have used the word recognition skills of phonics (how does it sound?), structural analysis (what are its parts?), and context clues (semantic cues—does it make sense? and syntactic cues—does it sound right?). More than likely, you use these skills every time you read.

We have written this book to help you recognize the reading skills you use and learn some new ones, and then learn strategies to teach them to your students. For each of the word recognition skills just listed we offer definitions and an overview, explain ways to teach it, provide strategies that teachers and students alike can use to reinforce the skill, and then present ways to assess student use of that specific skill. We also include information on supporting skills used by readers, such as previewing, visual clues, dictionary and reference skills, and how technology fits into the picture.

Because word recognition skills alone do not make up the act of reading, we go beyond word recognition to show how these skills work together to help readers reach the ultimate goal of reading—comprehension. We talk about how fluency and writing aid in improving comprehension and finally discuss how to incorporate all these reading skills and strategies throughout the curriculum in everything you teach.

Today's political climate has provided additional incentives for beginning teachers to have a strong base of knowledge concerning reading and word recognition. With the public's increasing focus on literacy, first-year teachers are just as likely to be asked difficult questions regarding students' achievement in reading and learning as are experienced teachers and principals. Teachers need to be secure in their knowledge about word recognition, phonics, reading achievement, and student assessment, and to be able to address these issues competently in relation to high-stakes testing, social promotion, and school accountability. With stricter standards in place, teachers must be prepared to face the challenge of meeting the needs of all of their students and be armed with appropriate instructional strategies. We believe this text will lay a strong foundation for you in both your understanding and teaching of word recognition skills to foster successful reading, comprehension, and learning.

We hope after reading this book you realize how much you do know about reading and that you will feel more prepared to pass on your reading expertise to your students. As the famous pediatrician Dr. Benjamin Spock once said, "You know more than you think you do."

Word RECOGNITION

Learning to read and becoming a lifelong reader involve learning how to recognize words. While the goal of reading is attaining meaning or comprehension, understanding text cannot take place until the reader can recognize words. The process used in reading and comprehending varies from person to person based on learning preferences and background knowledge, but readers share common strategies that are learned in school.

Good readers subconsciously check their own comprehension during the reading process. If Maya comes to a new word she does not recognize, she may skip over it without realizing it if meaning is not disrupted. In such cases, Maya does not need to know the word in order to understand what she is reading. Even if she does not derive meaning from knowing the word, Maya might be able to figure it out by reading the other words in the sentence, thus using *context clues*. Knowledge of the English language also may help Maya substitute another word that makes sense. Or, sounding out the word using knowledge of sound–letter relationships (phonics) may help.

Sometimes readers have words in their listening vocabulary that they have never seen in print, so when they sound out the word and say it aloud, they may recognize it. Readers also can apply their knowledge of root words, prefixes, or suffixes to determine an unknown word. If Maya still cannot figure out the word, the dictionary is another option. If after trying all of these clues, Maya does not know the word, she might ask someone for help. Although readers may intuitively use trial and error as **fluency** develops, teachers need to teach word recognition skills and strategies to assist in the reading process.

Reading educators use the following terms to describe these reading strategies:

- phonics (sound–letter relationships)
- structural analysis (word parts)
- context clues: semantic cues (meaning), syntactic cues (grammar)
- sight words and vocabulary
- supporting skills

The purpose of this unit is to define and explain the roles that word recognition skills play in the reading process; to provide strategies that teachers can use to teach these skills and strategies that students can use to become independent readers; and to offer ways to assess students' learning.

Defining Word Recognition

In *Becoming a Nation of Readers: The Report of the Commission on Reading,* Anderson, Hiebert, Scott, and Wilkinson (1985) state, "One of the cornerstones of skilled reading is fast, accurate word identification" (p. 36). Harris and Sipay (1990) define **word** recognition as "the ability to associate a printed word with its spoken counterpart either instantly or through some mediated process" (p. 432). In *The Literacy Dictionary: The Vocabulary of Reading and Writing,* published by the International Reading Association, Harris and Hodges (1995) define word recognition as "the process of determining the pronunciation and some degree of meaning of a word in written or printed form" (p. 283). Further, the skills they include in word identification are "phonic analysis, structural analysis, context clues, configuration clues, dictionary skills, and sometimes picture clues" (p. 282).

Good readers use all of these skills in tandem as they put the pieces of the puzzle together to make sense of the text. In teaching students how to read, teachers would be remiss if they did not fully embrace various components of **word recognition** and incorporate them in their instructional practices.

Why "Word Recognition" Instead of Simply "Phonics"?

Educators and parents are actively discussing the importance of phonics instruction. Phonics instruction is a big part of what people are asking for when they cry "back to basics!" **Phonics**, the sound–letter relationship, is an important piece in the word recognition puzzle, but it is only one piece. Phonics is one tool that readers need to recognize new words. It is a critical skill that helps beginning readers learn to read, and one that should be reinforced as they gradually encounter more complex texts. Teachers and students, however, need to see the whole picture—to make use of a variety of recognition skills and understand how they work together.

No matter what approach to reading instruction teachers use or whether they teach early childhood, elementary, middle school, secondary, special education, or English as a second language (ESL), teaching word recognition skills is a necessary element. Reinforcement of the appropriate word recognition skills should be emphasized and supported outside of reading classes and within content area reading. Teachers armed with a strong knowledge of word recognition skills and ways to strengthen students' use of the strategies will be better prepared to help readers increase their reading comprehension. Routman (1996) stated that "intensive, early phonics instruction does produce students with superior word-identification skills but it does not necessarily improve their comprehension" (p. 92). Therefore, teachers have to teach word recognition skills and to show students how to use those skills so they can derive meaning from what they read. Comprehension is the ultimate goal, and students need word recognition skills to reach the goal.

The Comprehension– Word Recognition Connection

The end product of recreational reading and reading from texts, as well as other types of reading, is comprehension. That is why people read: to comprehend. Among other goals, teachers offer instruction so students can read independently and want to read for recreation and pleasure. Students who have a good grasp of vocabulary and background knowledge are better equipped to become independent readers.

Comprehension and word recognition are highly related. Knowledge and use of vocabulary and other word recognition skills are effective predictors of comprehension ability (Chall, 1983; Chard, 1995). A general definition of comprehension is constructing meaning from written text. This certainly includes much more than decoding words. Meaning must be constructed from interaction with written text. Consider this: A person consists of more than a collection of bones, skin, and organs, although those are certainly important. Likewise, comprehending entails more than simply decoding written text, although the ability to decode unknown words is important. Comprehension combines many skills that lead to interacting with and understanding text. Teachers must have

a working knowledge of word recognition skills because comprehension difficulties often arise from inadequate application of these skills.

One way to determine if a reader has trouble with word recognition is to
administer an **informal reading inventory (IRI)**. An informal reading inventory
is an individually administered method of assessing approximate reading levels
first used in the 1940s. Harris and Hodges (1995) define it as "a graded series
of passages of increasing difficulty to determine students' strengths, weaknesses, and strategies in word identification and comprehension" (p. 116). (See the
discussion of IRIs later in this unit.)

A more informal means of determining whether a word recognition problem is causing a breakdown in comprehension is to have a student read aloud a
passage at the appropriate grade level. If the reader makes many word recognition errors that change the meaning, the student may have difficulty with word
recognition. Errors that do not change meaning, such as substituting "the" for
"this" or "that," generally are not considered critical when decoding, as fluent
readers often substitute synonyms for the exact word without altering meaning.

If readers have little or no difficulty decoding or reading aloud a text but are
unable to retell it or to answer questions about the content, they likely have a
comprehension breakdown not caused by decoding or word recognition problems. Johns (1986) stated, "a student who pronounces words accurately but
fails to reconstruct meaning from the printed page is merely calling words or
barking at print" (p. 118). Other strategies, such as predicting, previewing, and
questioning the text are then needed to help strengthen comprehension. For
specific strategies to help students build comprehension see "Increasing
Comprehension" in Unit 4.

Readers generally have difficulty comprehending until they are able to read
without having to focus on decoding. **Automaticity** (Samuels, 1988) describes
the ability to read without having to labor at decoding. Readers cannot easily
attend to meaning until decoding becomes automatic, done at a subconscious
level. When readers are struggling to decode, reading usually breaks down.

As important as decoding is to word recognition, vocabulary based on prior
knowledge and experience is also important in supporting comprehension. In
reality, separating word recognition ability and vocabulary from comprehension
is difficult. A reader who does not know how to decode with fluency, does not
have a vocabulary adequate for reading a given passage, and does not know how
to apply other word recognition skills will have great difficulty comprehending.
Holmes (1965) talked about a **substrata theory** in which he hypothesized that
comprehension ability and vocabulary or word recognition could not be separated. Therefore, the plot thickens regarding how teachers might help students
develop and strengthen their word recognition abilities. Strategies to help students build fluency will be offered in Unit 4.

Helping Students Make
the Reading Connection

 eachers must help students make the connection between word recognition and comprehension. One strategy to help readers who are still in the
acquisition stage of reading is to offer interesting literature at their level.

In helping readers choose a book, the teacher can show children how to use Veatch's (1966) **rule of thumb**. While reading a 100-word passage, readers put down one finger each time they come to a word they do not know. If they put down all four fingers and their thumb, the passage is too difficult for them. The rule-of-thumb strategy suggests that if readers make more than five meaning-changing mistakes per 100 words or about a page, they are either reading texts that are too difficult for them or they lack adequate word recognition skills. Often, students choose books that are too difficult for them if they are interested in the topic. Shel Silverstein books *Where the Sidewalk Ends* and *A Light in the Attic* are examples. Many children who read these books struggle over the vocabulary but still enjoy the challenge of reading his poetry for fun and enjoyment. Readers do not necessarily have to discard challenging books—they should have the freedom to pick up and try books they want to read regardless of the difficulty. Being conscious of the difficulty level, however, tells them they can choose easier books if they wish to read more easily. Teachers should provide a variety of easy and interesting books and other materials from which students can learn, model, practice, and apply word recognition strategies and skills to assist their comprehension and fluency in reading.

Comprehension is connected to the desire to read. The more students read, the more they want to read. The more they want to read, the better readers they become. Teachers can teach, practice, and review specific strategies and techniques with students to aid in comprehension. This book offers many specific strategies to tie word recognition skills to comprehension.

Assessing Word Recognition Skills

E ducators have to demonstrate accountability for student learning through a variety of assessment formats. Assessment is not necessarily a separate activity but, rather, is a tool to guide instruction and to inform. Assessment helps teachers determine students' strengths and needs, helps teachers plan instruction and monitor student progress, and provides feedback.

Many tools are available for assessing word recognition. Specific strategies and their specific uses will be included for each word recognition skill discussed throughout the book. The following assessment tools are effective for assessing most word recognition skills.

INFORMAL READING INVENTORY (IRI)

Many commercially prepared IRIs are available, each slightly different. In addition, many basal reading series have their own version of an IRI. Most IRIs include more than one reading passage at each level, used for further testing, and they focus on assessing oral reading skills, silent reading, comprehension in both oral and silent reading (by use of questions and/or retellings), and capacity/listening comprehension. Reading levels such as independent, instructional, frustration, and listening comprehension may be determined for each child.

By systematically marking miscues (errors), a teacher can determine specifically a student's strengths and areas of need. When meaning (comprehension) breaks down while a student reads a graded passage, the teacher may ascertain whether the student has the skills to figure out unknown words. If the skills are not evident, teaching strategies may reinforce specific word recognition skills. Likewise, a teacher may use the results of an IRI to find out which strategies students are using on their own to keep the meaning/comprehension ongoing.

Figure 1.1 shows a portion of an IRI (Flynt & Cooter, 2000, p. 23) that a student has read aloud. The student's miscues are marked. Most published IRIs have similar marking systems for text or word lists read aloud.

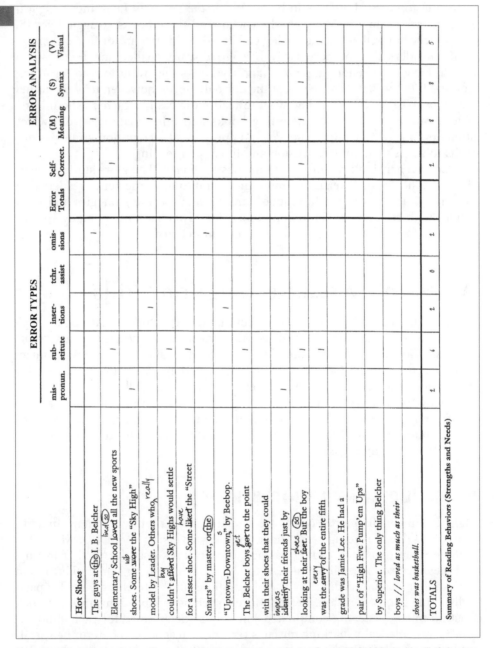

FIGURE 1.1

Sample IRI passage and marked miscues.

From *Reading Inventory for the Classroom,* 4th Ed., by Flynt and Cooter. Copyright © 2001 by Merrill (Columbus, OH). Reprinted with permission.

RUNNING RECORD

A **running record** is an individually administered reading assessment, which allows teachers to use any text for analysis. Clay (1993) defines this assessment as "a neutral observation task, capable of use in any system of reading, and recording progress on whatever gradient of text difficulty has been adopted by the education system" (p. 6). It is a method for recording errors (miscues) a student makes while reading orally with the miscues then analyzed using Clay's three cueing systems: semantic cues (does it make sense?), syntactic cues (does it sound right?), and visual cues (does it look right?). Many teachers like using this type of assessment because they do not need additional materials. Only the child's copy of the printed text and a sheet of paper (although additional forms are available) are necessary to take a running record.

By using gradient texts already in the classroom, such as a basal reading series or leveled benchmark books, a teacher will be able to establish three levels of difficulty for the child: "easy text or instructional text or hard text" (Clay, 1993, p. 23). (Instructional text is material that students can read with a little help from the teacher.) As with the IRI, the marking system is user-friendly. After analyzing the child's miscues, a teacher can determine the student's strengths, areas of need, and whether the student has attained meaning or comprehension.

A *quantitative evaluation* reveals the number and type of miscues or corrections a reader has made. A *qualitative evaluation* requires that the teacher observe the reading behavior and determine if the student uses fix-up strategies or word recognition skills in the reading process. This qualitative component of a running record helps a teacher evaluate how the "child gathers up cues from the . . . meaning of the message" (Clay, 1993, p. 22). As the teacher reviews the running record and analyzes the miscues the child has made while reading, the teacher thinks about whether the child possibly has used other cues such as context clues or background information.

Figure 1.2 shows an example of text on which a running record could be given. The miscues are indicated and placed next to the text for ease in comparing the lines of text with the marking system. The figure includes a brief explanation of the marks.

CLOZE PROCEDURE

The **cloze procedure**, originated by Taylor (1953), is used to determine how well a reader interacts with the text. This was defined as a "method of estimating reading difficulty by omitting every *n*th (usually fifth) word in a reading passage and observing the number of correct words a reader can supply . . . by using the surrounding context" (Burns, Roe, & Ross, 1996, p. 700). Choate, Enright, Miller, Poteet, and Rakes (1995) contend that "the cloze format offers the most practical approach to assessing application-level word recognition skills since it incorporates comprehension into the process but is not as time consuming as other in-context techniques" (p. 131).

Because this is a systematic deletion of words, a student may need some in-depth instruction in how to complete a cloze procedure effectively. Most students are used to focusing only on vocabulary words or "important" words rather than a systematic deletion of words.

*An example
of a running
record.*

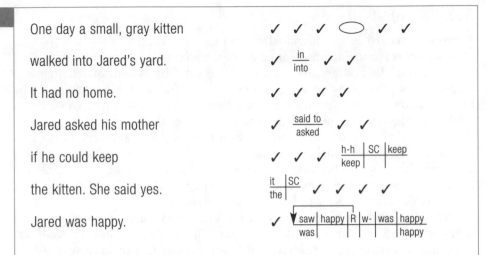

One day a small, gray kitten   ✓ ✓ ✓ ⬭ ✓ ✓

walked into Jared's yard.   ✓ in/into ✓ ✓

It had no home.   ✓ ✓ ✓ ✓

Jared asked his mother   ✓ said to/asked ✓ ✓

if he could keep   ✓ ✓ ✓ h-h/keep | SC | keep

the kitten. She said yes.   it/the | SC ✓ ✓ ✓ ✓

Jared was happy.   ✓ saw/was | happy | R | w- | was | happy/happy

Line 1—**gray** was omitted and indicated by a circle—a meaning-changing miscue

Line 2—**in** was substituted for into—a nonmeaning-changing miscue

Line 3—no miscues

Line 4—**said to** was substituted for **asked**—a meaning-changing miscue (a statement instead of a question)

Line 5—started to say **have** but self-corrected (SC) to **keep**

Line 6—**it** was substituted for **the**—child realized it did not make sense and self-corrected (SC)

Line 7—read **saw happy** for **was happy**—realized it did not make sense, repeated **w,** and finished with the correct words **was happy**

In watching the reader and looking back over the records, the teacher determined that the child was using semantic cues in line 7 because meaning helped the child self-correct. This is an example of the qualitative components of running records.

Analysis of a cloze should help a teacher make informed decisions about appropriate materials to use with a child for instruction. In analyzing the cloze, the teacher also might discover independent and frustration levels. Like the running record discussed above, a cloze may be administered with materials already in use in the classroom, such as leveled books or a basal reading series. Commercially prepared cloze passages are also available.

Figure 1.3 shows an example of a partial teacher-constructed cloze using the story *Flat Stanley* by Jeff Brown (p. 26). Directions for how to construct a cloze are described in Unit 2. To score this cloze, count the exact word replacements the student makes and multiply by 7 for the cloze percentage (divide 100% by 14 blanks for 7 points each). Scores below 40% indicate that the text is too difficult, scores 40%–60% are at the students' instructional reading level, and scores above 60% might be easy or appropriate for recreational reading. If the student made eight correct substitutions, the score would be 56% (8 × 7 = 56) and the teacher could assume that the student would be able to read this story with some help.

FIGURE 1.3

An example of a teacher-constructed cloze.

    Three boys came up to Arthur and invited him to join them for a hot dog and some soda pop. Arthur _____ the spool wedged in _____ fork of the tree. _____ did not notice, while _____ was eating the hot _____, that the wind was _____ the string and tangling _____ about the tree.

The _____ got shorter and shorter, _____ Stanley did not realize _____ low he was until _____ brushed his feet, and _____ it was too late. _____ got stuck in the _____. Fifteen minutes passed before Arthur and the other boys heard his cries and climbed up to set him free.

Answers:

left	he	it	leaves
the	dog	string	then
He	blowing	but	He
		how	branches

CHECKLIST

In assessment, a **checklist** is a "list of specific skills or behaviors to be marked off by an observer as a student performs them" (Harris & Hodges, 1995, p. 28). Teachers might find using an observation checklist helpful because it enables teachers to know where students are developmentally and to track students' progress. The checklist is an informal assessment instrument and targets specific behaviors to be observed over time.

    Commercially prepared checklists are available for basically every concept of reading development. Some basal reading series also include checklists to assess students' progress through leveled material. A teacher, however, may want to prepare a checklist specifically for the literacy behaviors to be observed in a given classroom. Copies of completed checklists can be kept in individual students' folders.

    Like anecdotal records, checklists may be cumulative and should drive instruction. Results might be recorded using yes/no, a Likert scale, or a similar rating device. After looking carefully at the ratings, this assessment may be used to group students for small-group instruction. By using a checklist such as that shown in Figure 1.4, a teacher may identify phonics skill areas in which a student is excelling or deficient. Analysis of the completed checklist might indicate that a student (or small group of students) needs instruction in decoding. Figure 1.4 shows an example of a checklist a teacher might use at the first-grade level, followed by an explanation.

FIGURE 1.4

*Phonics
checklist for
first-grade
level.*

SKILL AREA—PHONICS	1 Oct 10	2 Nov 7	3 Dec 3	4 Jan 8
Initial consonants	X	X	X	
Middle consonants	I	P	P	
Final consonants	P	X	X	
Short vowel sounds				
Long vowel sounds		I	P	

In this brief example, the teacher has observed or tested the student in specific sound identification and marked "X "for "learned during the time period or continued to master," "I" for "introduced," "P" for "making progress," or blank for skills not yet practiced. Some teachers like to date the information, and others simply check off the skills or concepts.

ANECDOTAL RECORD

Anecdotal records are informally written observations by teachers of individual students' social, literacy, or other behavior. Records usually are kept over a planned period of time. Typically, only the facts, as observed, are recorded. Often these records are followed by an analysis of the recorded facts. The analysis and/or interpretation of the reasons for the behavior are done after several observed episodes. These facts are recorded on gummed notes, index cards, gummed address labels, or other small pieces of paper, and placed in an individual student's folder. Anecdotal records may be used to observe social behavior as well as literacy behavior. Clay (1993) indicated, "Observations which lead us to modify our instruction are particularly appropriate in the formative stages of new learning, as in beginning reading, [and] beginning writing" (p. 3). Because anecdotal records are ongoing, a teacher may have accumulated a lot of useful information about a student by the end of a school year. This information is helpful in guiding instruction throughout the year. By observing and recording reading behaviors, a teacher is able to note students' abilities to use word recognition skills.

Although anecdotal records can be beneficial for describing students' reading behaviors in short phrases, they may become cumbersome to manage. One suggestion is to keep handy a sheet of gummed mailing address labels, perhaps on a clipboard. As teachers circulate around the room, they can record quick comments as they watch the students. Labels are also effective during conferences with students or small-group discussions. Teachers can easily peel off the labels and attach them to the individual child's reading or teachers' folders. By conference time, teachers often have accumulated several notes with important information. Anecdotal records should be kept confidentially with other assessment information. Figure 1.5 shows an example of anecdotal records.

FIGURE 1.5

10/25 Kathy used decoding strategy for initial consonant sound while reading science text in class	10/25 John struggling with using prediction strategy to figure out unknown words—may need some additional help
10/28 Sally reading with fluency aloud in SS at grade level passage—great improvement	10/29 Evan check hearing test, does not seem to respond to all sounds in listening center

Anecdotal records.

QUESTIONS ABOUT CONTENT

Another method teachers can utilize to assess students' ability to use word recognition skills "involves asking students questions about the words and word elements in a passage after they read orally or silently" (Choate et al., 1995, p. 131). Teachers can ask questions such as, "Why do you think Lucas said he never returned to his friend's house?" or "How could you tell Lucas was angry?" or "What does the word 'aggravated' mean?" By asking questions, a teacher can find out what word recognition skills students are able or not able to use when trying to determine unknown words.

RETELLINGS

Teachers can glean important information from students' abilities to use word recognition skills through **retelling**. After students have read a story or passage, the teacher asks the students to explain what happened in the story. Harris and Hodges (1995) state, "The purpose of including retelling in miscue analysis is to gain insight into the reader's ability to interact with, interpret, and draw conclusions from the text" (p. 220). For example, if Tiffany read a story silently about a boy who loved his horse, yet when she was retelling the story, she talked about a house, the teacher would know that Tiffany was not using semantic cues to realize that she was reading about a horse.

WRITING

An often untapped but effective way to assess students' knowledge and direct use of word recognition skills is to have children write. When children first put words together, they are demonstrating "what they know about sound sequences, visual patterns, graphophonic [or relationships, and meaning]" (Routman, 1996, p. 8). For example, if Adam writes "piktr" for the word "picture," the teacher can see that he is matching the sounds he hears with the letters he has learned to associate with those sounds. Or if Jen writes, "I want a ball red" instead of "I want a red ball," the teacher can see that Jen needs help with syntactic cues or grammar and sentence structure. The way children write gives teachers clues concerning what skills students have mastered and which ones require strengthening.

The purpose of assessing students' use of word recognition skills is to guide instruction. When teachers perceive that students are lacking in certain areas, they can provide further instruction and practice to help them strengthen those skills. Assessment and effective instruction go hand-in-hand as teachers help students develop word recognition skills in order to become independent readers.

Breaking It
DOWN

A LOOK AT MAJOR WORD RECOGNITION SKILLS

As discussed in Unit 1, word recognition involves the use of major word recognition skills such as phonics, structural analysis, context clues including semantic cues and syntactic cues, and sight words and vocabulary. Putting all these skills together to derive meaning from text is what reading is all about. In this unit, each of these areas will be defined and explained. Strategies for both teachers and students are included, with specific examples for how to teach and assess each skill.

2.1 Phonics: How Does It Sound?

WHAT IS PHONICS?

Phonics is the relationship between sounds and symbols used in reading and writing. It ties sounds with alphabetic representations to enable comprehension. For much of the 20th century, the issue of phonics in reading and writing instruction had both an educational and a political focus, according to the Position

Statement of the International Reading Association (1997b). This IRA statement contends that, "Phonics instruction, to be effective in promoting independence in reading, must be embedded in the context of total reading/language program" (p. 2). Therefore, educators have to understand how phonics contributes to the larger picture of word recognition.

An important related term when discussing phonics is **phonemic awareness**, "an insight about oral language and in particular about the segmentation of sounds that are used in speech communication" (International Reading Association, 1997a, p. 2). Phonemic awareness encompasses the recognition that words are made up of sounds and that sounds in words can be manipulated, as well as the ability to determine if words sound alike or different (including rhymes and alliteration). It does not include knowing what letters spell the sounds. That is the role of phonics (matching sounds to letters). For example, in the word "bat" the sounds heard are /b/ /a/ /t/. Students with phonemic awareness are able to hear and distinguish between the three sounds. Similarly, they hear one sound in the consonant digraph /ch/ as in "chain." It is an awareness about the oral sounds that sets the stage for acquiring the sound–letter relationship.

According to the IRA Position Statement (1997a), "Phonemic awareness predicts reading success" (p. 3). Young children who have developed phonemic awareness can make the connection between sounds and speech, then alphabetic print, and finally reading. When they see a "b," they make the /b/ sound. The alphabetic writing system is unlocked. This is a critical time in the emergent stage of reading for teachers to check to see if their students have phonemic awareness as they begin working with letters, reading, and writing. If students have developed a sense of hearing different sounds, they should be able to pick out similar sounds. Once they can pronounce a variety of sounds and are successfully hearing different sounds, they can begin learning representations associated with the sounds used orally in the English language. Phonemic awareness focuses clearly and solely on sounds. Once students can link letter knowledge and sounds, they move into phonics.

Phonics connects phonemic awareness (this sound is /a/) and alphabet knowledge (this is an "a"). Teaching phonics helps children to connect a specific sound with a letter or letters, such as blends and digraphs (discussed later in Section 2.1). Thus, teaching children to put together their own knowledge of sounds with English standard graphic representations is a part of phonics instruction. Adams (1990) states, "The goal of teaching phonics is to develop students' ability to read connected text independently" (p. 272). Knowledge of phonics gives students a tool to use rapidly and independently to figure out unknown words. Phonics requires that students convert speech sounds to letters and then put those sounds and letters together to form words.

For readers at all levels of reading proficiency, matching letters or combinations of letters with sounds is crucial to uncovering words and meaning. Good readers use phonics to sound out words or word parts by connecting them with meaning, with known words or other word parts, or with word analysis of letters and clusters of letters.

Effective reading teachers support the importance of phonics knowledge, practice, and teaching, but the way to teach phonics is often debated and misunderstood. Teaching phonics in context is generally considered more valuable in helping readers understand the connection of letters and sounds to words and meaning. When students are presented with texts that are interesting and meaningful, they are more motivated to figure out ways to read and be involved with the text. Routman (1991) suggests that children are more successful in learning phonics when they move from oral sounds to visual letters rather than a traditional practice of matching letters to sounds. In the sound-to-letter connection, students are actually moving from something with which they are familiar to something new. This progression supports an important learning principle of moving from the known to the unknown.

For example, when 3-year-old Maddison wanted to label the picture she had drawn of her mother, she asked her mother, "How do you write the 'mmm' sound?" She was naturally trying to apply a phonics skill by matching a sound (known) with a letter symbol (unknown). Maddison quickly learned that the letter "m" represented the /m/ sound. The oral understanding (phonemic awareness) preceded the graphic understanding. Because Maddison was including the word *mom* on her picture, the phonics application had a meaningful context. This also illustrates the connection of phonemic awareness to reading and writing.

Although how and how much phonics instruction should take place remains controversial, teaching beginning readers the sound–letter relationships has to be a part of reading instruction. Providing an environment rich with oral language, books, authentic print, reading, and writing opportunities support students' meaningful use of phonics and other word recognition skills, according to many research studies (Gambrell, 1996; Goodman, 1986; Graves, 1991; Routman & Butler, 1996). Students taught to use phonics and other word recognition skills in context will make greater progress in becoming independent readers.

According to Cunningham (cited in Robinson, McKenna, & Wedman, 1996, p. 76), "We are always going to have some phonics instruction and that we [teachers] have a responsibility to influence the form that instruction takes." In a summary of the research concerning the word recognition process of young readers, Cunningham warned that teaching phonetic rules or the letter by-letter sounding-out process does not support the recent brain theories. She describes a process wherein the brain looks at spelling patterns or letter combinations that match sounds the reader already knows, and uses that information to decode words rapidly. Cunningham urges teachers to help readers become familiar with sounds, spelling patterns, meaning, and context to assist the brain in simultaneously blending information for fluency.

HOW IS PHONICS TAUGHT?

Educators have varying viewpoints, often emotionally expressed, concerning the most effective way to teach phonics. According to Richgels, Poremba, and McGee (1996), the traditional teaching of phonics has been through extensive skill and drill in a direct instructional approach. They, as many other educators, have suggested beginning phonics instruction using meaningful texts while involving students with sounds, letters, reading, and writing. As children are exposed to books or other print, they begin learning that symbols on the page represent sounds and words, and that those representations are linked to the pictures they see on the page.

A more currently accepted approach to phonics instruction has been to "provide children a balanced, eclectic program involving both reading skill instruction and immersion in enriched literacy experiences" (Baumann, Hoffman, Moon, and Duffy-Hester, 1998, p. 636). Students first learn sound–letter relationships and then how to apply decoding skills to words while working with a variety of texts. Baumann et al. also found that a systematic approach to phonics instruction in the context of reading with writing worked best—following systematically the developmental levels of children but not in absolute, isolated sequential steps.

Cunningham (cited in Robinson, McKenna, & Wedman, 1996) also discussed the importance of teaching phonemic awareness and phonics as part of word recognition. From the research she gathered, she concluded that children develop strong word recognition abilities through

- a rich background in literacy development from home environment
- phonemic awareness
- application of strong decoding skills to learn sight words
- practice in dividing words into chunks or syllables
- continued reading and the development of fluency
- concurrently writing and learning to write
- the support of invented spellings in the writing process.

Teachers must know the basics for teaching phonics as a word recognition strategy because readers can apply phonics rules at any time to assist them in decoding.

Phonics instruction is most important for teachers in early childhood (birth through age 8). Yet, teachers in elementary, middle school or junior high and, yes, even secondary education must understand the process and know some phonic strategies to assist their struggling readers or for teaching content-specific vocabulary. ESL students at every level need phonic support from teachers. Students with learning disabilities or who are developmentally delayed often benefit from teachers' incorporating phonics into reading instruction. **Content-area reading** teachers can make successful use of phonics connections as they introduce new terms. Consequently, all teachers need to learn about phonics and how to teach in a guided, interactive, and integrated approach.

A natural sequence for teaching beginning readers progresses developmentally from learning the sound–letter association to the more complex concept of understanding the sounds in words. We suggest that teachers become aware of the five general stages that students move through in learning to read with comprehension related to phonics and related rules as a word recognition skill: emergent literacy, phonemic awareness, phonics instruction, phonics generalization, and phonics application. The following sections will provide a foundation for understanding the developmental sequence in learning to use phonics as a word recognition skill.

EMERGENT LITERACY

As the term suggests, *emergent literacy* refers to the time from birth (or possibly before) until the child becomes ready for formal instruction in reading. Cecil (2001) suggests that parents and teachers can support emerging literacy in all young children by reading and talking to them or pointing out characteristics of print such as moving a finger from left to right while reading a story aloud. During the emergent literacy stage, children begin to hear sounds and develop speech, tell stories and pretend to write, and begin to notice some print conventions. Indicators that literacy acquisition is developing include an understanding that reading is enjoyable and important, stories begin at the front and end at the back, print is read from the left to the right, signs such as "McDonald's" can give us information, letters or symbols represent things or "words," and learning to say new words helps children ask questions or give information. Although this stage usually is thought of as pre-K, many students who come to kindergarten are still in the emergent literacy stage. If students have been in environments where little talk or reading occurs, teachers may have difficulty laying the foundation for reading.

Upon entering his kindergarten classroom, Clay told his teacher that his mommy had read him a story about Clifford the dog (*Clifford* books by Norman Bridwell). He explained that Clifford was "a big red dog and he lived with Emily and they played together, but Clifford was very big and sometimes got into trouble, but they got home, and Clifford's name started the same way his own name did and he had a dog, too, but not that big!" Clay obviously has had a literacy-rich background. He spoke a long sentence, used several adjectives to describe Clifford, and talked in the past tense. He connected the "Cl" in Clifford to the "Cl" in Clay, noticing the sound–letter relationship and the letter–symbol similarity. He retold the story with a beginning, middle, and ending. Clay is on track for learning to read.

Katie came in immediately behind Clay, and the teacher asked her what she did last night. Katie replied, "Eat cookie." The teacher asked what else she did, and Katie said, "TV." Katie needs more exposure to language. Teachers can help students such as Katie by frequently reading aloud picture books and easy-to-read texts, using **big books**, and modeling reading strategies. Modeling and providing more literacy encounters might include moving a pointer across the words and turning the pages while reading; playing a record player or tape with songs and stories; labeling items in the room and at home, such as the desk and sink; drawing, pretend writing, and painting in the writing center; singing songs and chanting nursery rhymes; and talking one-on-one and in small groups. Providing more exposure to oral and written language will help the emergent learner.

PHONEMIC AWARENESS

Phonemic awareness, as introduced earlier, refers to the recognition that words are made up of sounds, the knowledge that sounds in words can be manipulated, and the ability to determine if words sound alike or different. Children with phonemic awareness can make the sounds not only in isolation but also in words. Awareness of sounds does not mean the students connect the sounds to the letters yet. Phonemic awareness begins with hearing individual sounds and moves to hearing sounds blended together, then being able to put together or pull apart sounds. Clay, in the example above, heard the "cl" blend.

Because developing phonemic awareness in young children has become widely accepted as a necessary precursor to reading success, identifying instructional strategies to support this stage is important. Yopp (1992) suggests singing songs, playing games, creating rhymes and riddles, and reading books with alliteration to "facilitate children's ability to perceive that their speech is made up of a series of sounds . . . in the speech stream" (p. 699). She encourages teachers to include "sound matching activities, sound isolation activities, sound blending activities, sound addition or substitution activities, and segmentation activities" (p. 699). Language play and oral activities in group settings are crucial in developing phonemic awareness as they lead to a natural curiosity about letters/words and reading/writing. *Phonemic awareness is a key ingredient.*

The more familiar children become with the sounds (phonemes), the easier they can understand "how spoken language maps onto written language" (Griffith & Olson, 1992, p. 519). After students have developed phonemic awareness, teachers can begin phonics instruction. As students are refining their phonemic awareness and beginning some initial phonics learning, they become aware of the connection between the sounds they hear and the letters they see. As literacy emerges, students carry over the sound–letter relationship to read words and begin to sound out new words. Griffith and Olson point out that students can memorize letters and corresponding sounds; however, the transition to phonics and then to reading and writing is delayed if they are not able to isolate sounds in the context of words. Phonemic awareness is key. If phonemic awareness is present, the connection between the sounds and the graphic representations will transition easily into phonics instruction.

Strengthening phonemic awareness for students should be a primary concern for teachers in pre-K through first grade and for teachers working with ESL, special needs, language-delayed, or speech delayed students at any level. The Committee on the Prevention of Reading Difficulties in Young Children stated that phonemic awareness is "the key to understanding the logic of the alphabetic principle and thus to the learnability of phonics and spelling" (Snow, Burns, & Griffin, 1998, p. 1).

In her kindergarten class, Miss Emily began each morning with a listening song. She sang (to the tune of "The Muffin Man"), "Do you know a kitten's sound, kitten's sound, a kitten's sound? Do you know a kitten's sound? Say the sound with me." The children made the "meow" sound with her. The teacher continued with other sounds such as car horn, whistle, lion, and puppy. By helping the children expand their repertoire of sounds they were able to make, Miss Emily was preparing them for future phonemic awareness with letters and words. Next they sang three familiar rhymes together. Finally, the teacher read *Mrs. McNosh Hangs Up Her Wash,* by Sarah Weeks. They stopped and talked about words that sounded alike in the story and added them to a chart of sound-alike words from the story.

Later in the morning during center time, Miss Emily provided additional listening and speaking opportunities for strengthening phonemic awareness. In the listening center the children put on headphones connected to the tape player and listened and sang additional rhyming songs. The art center featured a clothesline and clothespins where children could hang pictures they had drawn of the rhyming objects from the morning story (such as bone and phone) or make up their own rhyming pairs. In the reading center children retold the story from the big book to each other and shared their favorite part of the story. While the children were doing this, the teacher worked one-on-one, giving a rhyming sounds survey.

The assessment the teacher gave consisted of a page with rows of pictures. She carefully explained that she wanted to see if the student could find the pictures that sounded alike. She gave an example from the morning story: "Do you remember Mrs. McNosh? She hung up her wash—the shirts and skirts. These words sound alike because they have the /irts/ sound. When I say and point to each picture, you point and repeat it. At the end of the line, you will circle the two pictures that sound alike."

Miss Emily began the test with "boy, chair, toy." Similar tests usually are available with published curricula or through school districts, or the teacher can construct them, to determine the extent to which students can hear the rhyme. This is also important for later, more complicated word recognition skills, understanding "onsets" (the beginning of a word such as the /d/ in "dime") and "rimes" (the rest of the word such as /ime/ in "dime"). See the section on structural analysis for additional information.

Additional activities that are especially helpful in developing phonemic awareness include listening to sounds and identifying them, singing rhyming songs, reading and listening to poetry, chanting, choral reading, sorting objects or pictures by sounds or rhymes, and learning tongue twisters. An important component of phonemic awareness for teachers to target is to help children hear and distinguish between different sounds. Environmental sounds are a good place to start, as in listening and making animal sounds, vehicle sounds, music, and noises they hear outside. Then, listening to sounds in words such as their names or in nursery rhymes will help them hear the connection to sounds and letters later. This awareness is a strong foundation for learning and applying phonics.

PHONICS INSTRUCTION

Learning to read words is an integrated process, requiring readers to consider several things at once. **Decoding** words or uncovering the pronunciation is the primary goal of phonics instruction. Teaching phonics to children helps them to connect a given sound with a letter or letters. Readers first see the letters, and then they begin forming the letter sounds in their mind. The two processes work hand-in-hand. As readers are first attempting decoding, they may call out the sounds letter by letter as Tim did in saying his name /t/ /i/ /m/. More advanced readers in phonetic understanding would read pin as /p/ /in/ using the chunk /in/. **Chunking**, in this text, refers to the practice of looking at groups of letters together as units to assist in decoding words.

The letter-name stage of phonics instruction is based on the alphabetic principle or the understanding that each letter represents a sound. When first teaching children that letters are symbols and that each letter is associated with a sound, it usually is easier for them to learn the **consonants** first because most consonants have one sound. Routman (1991) suggests a teaching sequence beginning with consonants (beginning, ending, digraphs, middle, blends) and then **vowels** (long followed by short). The main difficulty readers have with reading letter sounds is with the vowels, a, e, i, o, u, and sometimes y. Because vowel letters each have several different sounds, they are more difficult than consonants for readers. Most readers have little difficulty with reading the long sounds of vowels because the sounds are the letter names. Readers have more difficulty with the short and r-controlled sounds (such as in "car").

One way of helping readers to learn the short vowel sounds is to tie the sounds to words. *Short a* sounds like the beginning sound of "apple." Having children draw an apple helps them remember the short "a" sound. *Short e* sounds like the beginning sound of "egg." *Short i* sounds like the beginning sound of "igloo." *Short o* sounds like the beginning sound of "octopus." *Short u* sounds like the beginning sound of "umbrella." Drawing each of these helps children to learn corresponding sounds.

Children typically begin identifying initial word sounds then move to ending and finally to all parts of the word. They probably will use the initial letter (sound) to represent the entire word in their writing. Kendall wrote under his picture of his dog, Tuffy, "m d t" (My dog Tuffy). As readers become more familiar with letters and sounds, patterns emerge. Later Kendall learned the chunk /og/ and changed his picture to say "mi dog tfe." In the beginning of the alphabetic stage, children will write and spell words by the sounds they hear.

A supporting concept that can help with word identification is *letter or symbol awareness*. Because the stages discussed here are not absolute and children learn at different rates in a sometimes varying sequence, some learning about the shapes or sizes of letters usually has emerged over time. Certainly by the time students are refining their phonemic awareness and beginning some initial phonics learning in sound–letter relationship, the teacher can introduce **configuration clues**, in which beginning readers use the outline or general shape of words to help them identify words. Thus, the shape and length of the word *elephant,* with three letters extending above the line of print (l, h, and t) and one part below (p) was once thought to provide the reader with a visual clue about the word. Now, configuration clues are not considered reliable means of building word recognition skills beyond the initial stages of learning to read (Harris & Sipay, 1990, p. 446).

An activity that is fun for children in the emergent stage of literacy development is to act out the configuration while spelling words. For example, a kindergarten teacher may have the students reach for the ceiling if the letter they are spelling is a tall letter above the middle, such as "h." Then the students are to place their hands on their hips for a letter such as "o." Finally, the teacher might have them squat when the letter goes below the line, such as "p." When the students put the letters together, they have their hands up, hands in the middle, and squat for "h o p."

Another configuration activity supporting tactile/kinesthetic learners could be to use licorice strips to form letters while saying the sounds. MacKinzie made the letter "s" out of a long piece of red licorice, saying /s/ and explaining this was her "snake." This is an example of bodily/kinesthetic in the **multiple intelligences** theory. (See the section on multiple intelligences in Unit 4.)

The question remains: How do I teach phonics to my students? As mentioned, beginning with specific consonants usually is a good choice. Some teachers prefer to teach all of the consonant sounds before moving to the vowel sounds. Other teachers prefer a more integrated approach, teaching some consonants and then some vowels so students can begin to make words on their own. The sequence may be determined by the school's curriculum, preference, or district. However, the suggestions below may help to answer the broader question of how to teach phonics in general.

Begin with Consonants

Consonants have a more consistent sound than vowels do. Some teachers find the letter(s)-of-the-week approach helpful. For example, Mrs. Raecker's class is studying "Bb." She begins circle time by writing a message on a sheet of chart paper. She writes at the top a "b." Betsy raises her hand quickly and says that her name begins with "B." The teacher compliments Betsy by saying it does, adds the "B" to the chart, and points out that we can hear the /b/ sound. Next Mrs. Raecker asks the class to join her in saying the "b" sound and Betsy's name. The teacher takes an additional moment to talk about the capital letter in Betsy's name. (Notice how the teacher integrated a rule in writing at this point.)

Now the teacher poses the question: What other things begin with the /b/ sound? She adds to the list all the words the children say: baby, bike, blue, boy, Brian, beaver, bird, bus, bed, doll. Then she says, "Let's think about the sound at the beginning of 'dad.'" She accents the /d/ sound in "doll" three times. Finally, she asks, "Does this sound the same?" The class responds with "No."

Using a **teachable moment,** Mrs. Raecker asks if anyone can take off the /d/ sound and replace it with the /b/ sound. Betsy raises her hand and shouts "bar." "Very good," the teacher replies, "and can anyone think of a bar on the playground?" Several children quickly identify the monkey bars. Next the teacher reads to the class *The B Book* by Dr. Seuss. Together the students add more "b" words to the chart.

Finally, Betsy is called to the front of the circle. The night before, she had taken home the mystery letter bag and filled it with "b" things from home (things beginning with the letter "b"). Now during circle time, Betsy describes the things she brought in and the class tries to guess what "b" things are in the mystery bag. Mrs. Raecker does not limit the children's experience with the letter "b" to circle time. Centers provide enrichment throughout the day. Below are some examples of the centers Mrs. Raecker uses to reinforce the letters the children are learning.

Writing Center: The children write "Bb" in different ways depending on their ability and interest. The teacher provides crayons, markers, pencils, and chalk, along with blank writing paper for children who are ready to write "b" words. The teacher has scattered around the table a few note cards with "b" words and pictures. Troy starts by copying some of these on his paper. He is familiar with writing and can associate words with pictures and use them to tell his own story. Megan, on the other hand, has had no previous experience with reading or writing until coming to kindergarten. She comes to the writing center and picks up a big pencil and a piece of paper with dotted lower and upper case "b's" for her to practice. Although the teacher finds independent exploration of letter formation the best way for children to practice writing, in Megan's case tracing is helpful and assists her fine-motor development.

Discovery Center: The teacher has a tub of odds and ends such as plastic bugs, buttons, toy cars, small stuffed bears, tiny balls, erasers of different shapes, blocks, and more. Children sort the items by things that begin with the letter "b" and things that do not. Chelse accumulates a number of items. When the teacher walks by, she asks Chelse to tell her the items in her "b" pile. Chelse shows her the ball, balloon, battery, and beetle (bug). The teacher asks her about one last item—a flower. Chelse looks at Mrs. Raecker and says "begonia." Chelse's family grows begonias, so she has had prior experience to draw upon.

Reading Center: The children are asked to find several alphabet books and several "b" books including Dr. Seuss's *The B Book* to reread. Some students read individually, and others read in pairs.

Art Center: The teacher provides sand, glitter, feathers, construction paper, sequins, and glue. The children create "b" pictures for their class book using the available supplies. When they finish, the teacher helps them write their word or sentence at the bottom of the page.

Kitchen Center: The children play dress up. The teacher labeled some of the special things the night before and added them to the center to help them see other "b" words in their life. She put "boots" on the shoe rack, a "broom" in the closet, a "bell" by the dinner table, pretend "bread, beans, bananas, beets" in the cupboard, and "bibs" on all of the "babies" in the "buggies."

Block Center: The children also practice their patterning by stacking the blocks that begin with the letter "b," like the black and blue blocks. The children stack the blocks until they fall over. The tallest pattern was the pattern of black, blue, black, blue because the black blocks were just a little bigger.

Consonant digraphs. Two consonants that work together to form one sound are called **consonant digraphs.** Sh, ch, kn, wh, and ph are examples of digraphs. Children do not have to memorize the term *digraphs* to understand the concept. Rather, teachers should concentrate on helping children identify the sound and be able to write the letter pattern. Centers can be used to give additional experience in hearing and speaking digraphs.

Another way for teachers to effectively teach digraphs is by modeling writing, sounding out words, and thinking aloud for children. A few weeks after the lessons on "b," Mrs. Raecker gathered her class on the carpet at the front of the room. She reread *The B Book* to the children, followed by **choral reading** of all of the words on the "Bb" chart now posted on the **word wall.** Next she asked the class to help her write a story about a big black bear. The teacher was reinforcing what the children had learned previously and tie it to a new concept. She began with the title, asking, "What should we have as the title for our story?" Kevin raised his hand and offered, "Ben the Big Black Bear." The teacher then asked Kevin to help her spell the title. "B-e-n," he replied. The teacher complimented Kevin on remembering how to spell his classmate's name and reinforced changing the "b" to "B." Then she continued, "After my space holder [holding up two fingers on the chart paper to represent the space between words], I write that little word we use a lot—t-h-e. Next I use my space holder again and write B-i-g."

The teacher continued writing the title of the story, modeling the sounds, then the letters, and then the symbol. When finished, she dropped down a line with her finger, indented a big space, and turned to the class again. "Now I want my story to say, 'Ben likes to sit in the shade.' Can you help me spell?" The children began, "B-e-n, don't forget your space holder, l-i-k-e-s, space, t-o, space, s-i-t, space, i-n, space, t-h-e, space." Then there was a pause. The children tried to think of a letter that makes the "sh" sound. The teacher accepted a few answers before calling on Shannon and asking her if she heard anything that sounds like part of her name. Shannon sounded out the two words (*Shannon* and *shade*) and announced that both words have the "sh" sound.

The class learned that two letters form the sound. The teacher asked Shannon for another sentence for the story. Shannon contributed, "Ben has sharp teeth." The teacher modeled saying the sounds, letters, and writing the symbols, plus reviewing the "sh" sound in "sharp." Teaching digraphs in context helped the students hear and see the sound–letter relationship.

Later Mrs. Raecker had the children think of other "sh" words, and they built a "sh" chart for their word wall. The "sh" chart is an example of an **onset** (a word family) and will be used again and again to draw children's attention to common parts of words. Word families, by onset or **rime**, can help children hear the rhyming sounds and learn word parts and affixes. Although **word families** has been used in different ways over time to label words that are similar in pattern or linguistically, more recently educators have tended to use the terms *onsets* and *rimes* to describe sets of words. The rime is at the end of the word, as in "ill" in bill, thrill, and trill, whereas the onset is at the beginning of the word, as in "br" in break, brown, and bread. Routman (2000) notes that 37 basic rimes can be used to make 500 words. As students learn rhyming words and begin to distinguish the sound–letter relationships, their understanding of phonics grows.

Consonant blends or clusters. Two or more consonants that work together to form more than one sound are called **consonant blends or clusters**. Str, st, br, fr, sn and sw are examples of blends. The examples given for individual letters and digraphs can be applied to teaching clusters or blends. Building new words can be a fun learning activity for teachers to illustrate clustering or blending letter sounds. For example: Begin with the word *wing* and have a volunteer tell the class what letter is needed to change *wing* to *swing*. Then try the word *well* to form *swell*. The children will begin hearing the "sw" sounds as they blend. Having the students try the same word-making exercise with *peak, pin, poke,* and *port* to form *speak, spin, spoke,* and *sport* will help them with the "sp" cluster.

Creating a paper plate cluster wheel can help students see how to make new words or how a cluster fits a variety of rimes. To create a simple wheel, cut a 3-inch pie wedge from a paper plate. Place it on top of another paper plate and fasten the two together with a paper fastener in the center.

On the top plate write the cluster, and on the bottom plate write a word part or rime in the open window, as illustrated. Spin the top plate around to a blank spot and write another word part or rime. Teachers can use these to check for mastery in pronouncing words using clusters.

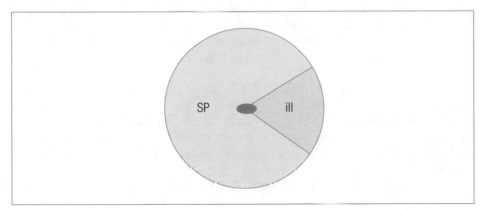

Teaching Vowels

The vowels are a, e, i, o, u, and sometimes y and w. Vowels represent short, long, or alternate sounds. Teachers differ in teaching long or short vowel sounds first. Those preferring to teach short vowels first believe the sounds are more regular, those preferring to teach long vowels first believe the sounds are easier because they say their names.

Short vowel sounds are more consistent. When introducing the short "a," teachers might begin with the word "ant." Other good words that begin with the short "a" include: and, apple, alligator, an, at, am. If the teacher has already introduced the consonants n, t, m, and l, the children probably are ready to work with word families or rimes.

Mr. Thompson introduced his first graders to the short "a" in ant. They read the big book *Effie,* by Beverly Allinson, and went through it page-by-page, circling the words with the short "a" sound. Mr. Thompson had taken apart the big book and laminated the pages, then reassembled the book and placed rings along the binding. This way he or the children could circle or underline parts of the story or words with a dry-erase marker and easily wipe it off with an eraser after they had finished.

Later the book was used in a center for children to practice on their own. The teacher then had the students recall all of the words they found in *Effie* with the short "a" sound and began making their "Aa" class chart. Then Mr. Thompson put the word "am" on a clean sheet of poster paper. He had the students read the word along with him three times. Then he asked if anyone could make a new word by adding a letter to "am" that they had already learned. Caitlin raised her hand and answered "ham!" This was followed by other students' suggestions until the teacher had written: ham, Sam, ram, dam, jam, Pam.

The teacher suggested that they try another short "a" pattern because they had done so well at making "am" words. This time they tried "at" and came up with cat, bat, fat, hat, mat, and sat.

Younger students benefit from making words that sound alike and connecting the sounds to letters and word parts. Older students also can benefit from this exercise in sound–letter relationships and patterns and also might benefit from learning the consonant–vowel–consonant (CVC) short vowel pattern to help them with bigger words such as "com" in "complete." Teachers should take care to introduce *rimes* and making words as both parts of words /h/ /a/ /m/ sounds blended together and onsets and rimes /h/ /am/.

Long vowel sounds usually are easier to remember because the vowel "says its name." The long "a" sound is found in the word "came." One rime that students can use for decoding (reading) or **encoding** (spelling) other words is "ame," which can be used to make dame, fame, game, lame, same, tame, and blame (using a cluster). One long vowel pattern that may be taught at this point is the consonant–vowel (CV) pattern (as in "me") or a stand-alone vowel (as in the pronoun "I"). Teaching long vowel sounds using word rimes will strengthen students' future use of the word recognition strategy described more fully in the section on syntax.

Teaching other vowel sounds and patterns can be integrated as children come in contact with words or discrete sounds within words. For example, when decoding "sky," the "y" has a long /i/, and in the word "sympathy," the first "y" is a short /i/ and the second "y" is a long /e/. Sometimes "w" joins with another vowel to create a glided vowel sound, as in "thaw" or "grow." Table 2.1 offers examples of the vowel sounds and patterns used most frequently. Teachers should determine the order or introduction of vowel sounds and patterns based upon their students' needs and abilities.

VOWEL SOUNDS OR PATTERNS	TYPE	EXAMPLES
CVC	short vowel	c<u>a</u>t, b<u>e</u>t, s<u>i</u>t, l<u>o</u>t, p<u>u</u>p
VC, VCC, VCCC	short vowel	<u>a</u>t, <u>e</u>bb, <u>i</u>tch
CV	long vowel	m<u>e</u>, s<u>o</u>, b<u>e</u>
VV	long vowel	m<u>ai</u>l, m<u>ea</u>t, def<u>ea</u>t, b<u>ee</u>, g<u>oa</u>t
VCe	long vowel	b<u>a</u>ke, b<u>i</u>ke, c<u>a</u>me, r<u>a</u>ge
Vr	r-controlled	f<u>ar</u>m, t<u>er</u>m, f<u>ir</u>m, s<u>or</u>t, t<u>ur</u>n
ə	schwa	<u>a</u>bove, sick<u>e</u>n, mel<u>o</u>n
VV	diphthong	<u>ou</u>ch, c<u>ow</u>, c<u>oi</u>l, b<u>oy</u>
VV	vowel digraph	f<u>oo</u>d, b<u>oo</u>k, c<u>oa</u>t, ch<u>ea</u>t

TABLE 2.1

Common vowel sounds and patterns with examples.

PHONIC GENERALIZATIONS

When teaching children to read, teachers often teach phonic generalizations. When a "p" and "h" are together, for example, they make the /f/ sound, and when a "k" is followed by an "n," the "k" is silent. Clymer (1996, reprinted from 1963) compiled a list of 45 commonly accepted phonic generalizations (see Appendix A) that may guide phonics instruction. In his classic study, he analyzed four sets of basal readers for the frequency of word usage correlated with the generalizations. From the application of generalizations, he reported the number of words conforming, number of exceptions, and percent of utility. These apply to a large number of words usually encountered in the primary grades.

Clymer cautions that because the English language does not always follow the generalizations, these words should be taught with great care and have limited use. Teachers can use this information when making decisions concerning which phonic generalizations to teach to their students. For example, middle school teacher Lori Breckner has a phonic generalizations wall. She lists the generalizations across the top and has the students look for words that fit the generalization. She also has a place for words that do not fit the generalizations.

The critical issue seems to be which generalizations to teach. With the growing interest by state legislatures to hold teachers accountable for teaching phonics, teachers must understand the "phonics rules." The extent to which the rules contribute to word recognition is determined by the context of the material. For example, when Mrs. Stone reads *Sheep in a Jeep,* by Nancy Shaw, to her students, she teaches students the generalization, "When two vowels go walking, the first one does the talking," as in cheap and meat. She goes on to explain to her students that the rule has exceptions, such as "great," and "chief," in which the second vowel is stressed. Mrs. Stone is teaching a phonic generalization in context as her students encounter words that fit the rule.

PHONICS APPLICATION

As readers encounter new words, one strategy they can call upon to help them identify a word is their understanding of phonics. Using their knowledge of sounds, letters, rimes, and word parts can help them decode unknown words. Phonics application gives readers another tool to uncover the written language or coding system for the English language. Symbols represent sounds. The process of decoding simply means breaking or interpreting the code, called *decoding*. Sounding out the word helps students identify the **phonemes** (sounds), blend them, and listen for auditory clues for words in their listening vocabulary. Children may benefit by repeatedly using books and materials that contain many words spelled like they sound. Cunningham (cited in Robinson, McKenna, & Wedman, 1996), describes the decoding process as:

> [W]hen readers come to unfamiliar words, they do a fast search through their cognitive word stores for similar words with the same letters in the same places. They then use these analogs to come up with a possible pronunciation, which they try out and cross-check with meaning. (p. 81)

Cunningham further explains that the brain does not apply the rules of decoding or phonics but, rather, detects patterns in words and rimes to figure out or decode the text. Practicing word families with students as part of phonics instruction will help them search for these routinely in unknown words. As readers come to unknown words, they may pronounce them incorrectly. Teaching them to decode or break down the word into parts they recognize will help. Readers might say the word letter-by-letter, sounding out each sound and blending them, as in /b/ /a/ /d/ for "bad." More experienced readers could look for word parts they recognize and add onsets to help them. An example is decoding "recalling" by /call/, adding /re/, and then /ing/ to form the word.

Using a piece of posterboard about 4 inches long by 1 inch wide, teachers can help students to decode words. Teachers demonstrate sounding out a word by sliding the cardboard marker across a word while modeling how to make the sounds and blend them to uncover the word. This can be seen readily when reading a big book or using the overhead projector. Students can replicate the process using a smaller marker and placing it over unknown words while they are reading, and sliding it across the letters from left to right while sounding out the letters or chunks. Saying the sounds and blending them plus looking for familiar chunks assists in the pronunciation of words. Older students can use their finger in place of a marker as a placeholder. Eventually, readers learn not to use a marker or their finger but instead use their eyes to slide across the word while blending sounds. Teaching students how to decode unfamiliar words through this method will carry through as the students develop fluency, encounter more complex text, and write.

Teachers should introduce decoding as they are teaching phonics and generalizations. While building words and rimes, the students should practice sounding out words and using decoding as a means of word recognition. Learning phonics and how to generalize phonics works well as a fix-up strategy in word recognition for good readers. Applying in context what they are learning will strengthen their reading abilities and word recognition skills.

Learning to write and using phonics as a word recognition strategy should go hand in hand. As students learn to spell and write words, they can use their understanding of phonics to help them figure out how to represent their speech in graphic form. Teaching letters and sounds together after students have developed phonemic awareness through reading and writing will strengthen the writing connection to phonics.

Mrs. Childers has her kindergartners first draw in the air a "B" (capital), then "b" (lower case). During each practice at "air writing," the children say the letter and the /b/ sound. Each time, they erase the letters and "air write" again until they have practiced the letters five times. Then the children "rainbow-write" the Bb combination on their lined paper: They carefully trace over the "B," then the "b," with a red crayon. On top of the red they trace orange, then yellow, green, blue, and purple. When they are finished, they have a rainbow of colors on each letter. Rainbow writing is good with tactile/kinesthetic learners because it reinforces their learning style. Finally, the children select "B" alphabet books or stories the teacher has found that contain many words beginning with the letter "b."

In this example, Mrs. Childers has her students write, read, and practice phonics learning at the same time. At the other end of the building in a fifth grade class, Mr. Watson is telling his students to use phonics strategies to sound out any words they do not know how to spell, while writing rough drafts of Old West stories for literature. As Maria writes her own exciting story about cowboys and cattle drives, she uses the spellings "cowboies" and "catel drivs." Later, while revising the stories, Maria and her classmates will go back and edit their texts, using the dictionary to check spellings. At both of these levels, kindergarten and fifth grade, letters and sounds work to develop or support word recognition skills while strengthening reading and writing.

Next, specific strategies are provided for teachers to use for phonics instruction and for students to use in phonics application. For each of the strategies given throughout the book, we have indicated the grade level(s) at which the strategy will work best: All, Primary, Intermediate, Middle, Secondary, ESL (English as a Second Language).

WHAT STRATEGIES CAN TEACHERS USE TO REINFORCE PHONICS?

BIG BOOKS AND CHILDREN'S LITERATURE

PRIMARY

Large-sized books, usually about 2 feet by 3 feet, allow the teacher to read aloud while the children look at the pictures and text, not possible with regular-sized children's books. Big books are wonderful for supporting oral language development of phonemic awareness and then connections to letters, words, pictures, and print. Using big books, teachers can reinforce the emergent literacy skills that some children bring to school and teach these skills to others who do not have a literacy background.

Teachers can begin with print awareness and conventions of print, such as reading from left to right and from top to bottom of the page, using a pointer or their index finger while reading aloud. They introduce their students to books through prediction exercises in which the children guess at the story based upon the book title and illustrations. The teachers make known that authors and illustrators use language to tell stories. Then, during shared reading experiences, teachers can ask students to identify letters and sounds, apply decoding strategies to figure out new words, or demonstrate new letter patterns.

PHONICS CHARTS

Words that students identify, preferably within the context of a story, are listed on a **phonics chart.** The lists consist of words and sometimes pictures with shared phonetic characteristics, such as "sh" in shop, shoe, dish, and wash. After reading the book *Is Your Mama a Llama?*, by Deborah Guarino, for example, the teacher might ask the students, "What words in this story rhyme?"

SOUND OF THE WEEK

One way to teach new sounds is to introduce a sound of the week, looking for examples in context. Children are asked to associate sounds with letters at the beginning of words they are familiar with or recognize in print. Teachers can display charts with words, pictures, and sounds. Using letter puppets or animal charts for the letter of the week is an interesting way to present sound/letter relationships. Using students' names as a starting point for the week personalizes the sound/letter connection (/m/ is the beginning sound in Maddison, mom, Mark, and Mrs. Marsch).

Benefits of using the letter-of-the-week approach include focusing on a specific letter, concentrating on finding the letter in context or working with a letter over time, and sharing resources with several teachers in a building. Proponents of this approach point out that each week highlights a letter to add to others when learning to read, write, and work with phonics. The biggest disadvantage to this approach is that children are not introduced to all of the letters until the 26th week of school. Teachers should not implement a sound-of-the-week strategy as the only means of working with sound/letter relationships.

MAKING WORDS

Students enjoy creating new words through rhyming, word sorts, and building words using a variety of materials such as magnetic letters, tiles, and tactile experiences (for example, writing words in sand or pudding, making words with dough). In the primary grades, teachers might use a pocket chart and place a word part on the right-hand side. Students take turns adding to or changing the initial letter to form new words. Working with word families teaches children how initial sounds can change words such as hat, cat, mat, sat, fat, bat, and pat.

In their book *Making Words: Multilevel, Hands-on Developmentally Appropriate Spelling and Phonics Activities,* Cunningham, Hall, and Heggie (1994) provide a variety of activities that show children how to make words. For example, the teacher gives each child individual cutouts of the letters *i, r s, k, t,* and *c,* then tells the children to make a one-letter word such as *I.* Then the teacher instructs them to make a two-letter word such as *is* or *it,* then a three-letter word such as *sit,* then a four-letter word such as *tick,* then a five-letter word such as *trick.* Finally the teacher asks students if they can make a big word using all six letters such as *tricks.*

VARIATION. Cunningham and Hall (1999) provide another example of making words, in which the teacher tells students how to turn a *hen* into a *cat.* The teacher asks the students to write the word *hen,* then tells them to change the *h* to a *p* to make the word *pen;* then to change the *e* to *i* to make the word *pin;* the *p* to an *f* to make *fin;* the *i* to an *a* to make *fan;* the *f* to a *t* to make *tan;* the *n* to an *r* to make *tar;* the *t* to a *c* to make *car;* the *r* to a *t* to make *cat.* The students now have changed a *hen* to a *cat.*

TRANSFORMATION

Another term used to describe the process of changing words, *transformation* might be more grade-appropriate terminology at the intermediate, middle school, or secondary level. Older students can be challenged to figure out the hen-cat transformation for themselves or to make up their own transformations.

INTERMEDIATE
MIDDLE
SECONDARY

RACING

Older students enjoy word games such as racing to see who can make the most words from the letters in "superstitious" (for example super, tissue, stir, sir, purse). The game begins with two teams having an equal number of students. The teacher places the key word on the overhead projector or chalkboard. The students begin making words using only the letters in the key word. After 1 minute the teacher calls "time" and the students stop writing. Team members combine their lists and total the words. Point values for words could differ based on the number of letters or syllables; for example, 1 point for 1–2-syllable words and 2 points for 3–4 syllable words. Teachers can devise variations.

INTERMEDIATE

ALPHABET BOOKS

To help students make connections between letters and their sounds, alphabet books can be useful. For example, students will learn to recognize, write, and say the letter "d." They draw pictures or cut out magazine pictures that start with the letter, such as dog, dinner, dish, dive, deck, dessert, desert.

PRIMARY

WORD WALLS

Many primary grade classroom walls are lined with words that students are learning. When a class is introduced to a new word, it is written on a slip and added to the wall. Words can be sorted alphabetically or by topics such as colors, days of the week, or number words. Usually the words remain on the wall all year. Content, thematic, or seasonal word wall words often are in a different location and are removed (some may be moved to the permanent word wall) after the study is completed. From their word wall, students can connect sounds in new words to words they are familiar with.

INTERMEDIATE

POSTERS

Word walls can be modified for use in middle schools and secondary school classes by creating posters with some of the basic generalizations and connecting them to new words the students are encountering in the content-area class

INTERMEDIATE
MIDDLE
SECONDARY

discussions, reading, or writing. Jennifer Cvitak has found that her high school science students have trouble memorizing new vocabulary until they are first able to pronounce the words correctly. With her knowledge of multiple intelligences theory, Ms. Cvitak concluded that these students are auditory learners. Other students in the same class who are visually dominant must see the written words. Using class charts (as a form of a word wall) could be helpful. Figure 2.1 shows a phonic generalization chart for a middle school or secondary level connected to a vocabulary chart, illustrating how phonics can assist older students. Notice how the teacher underlines the part of the word for the generalization application.

Hanging posters with familiar words will assist older students who are struggling with reading, by transferring decoded sounds, word parts, suffixes, or prefixes to new words. Vocabulary and spelling lists may contain special sound patterns and letter configurations. Teaching mini lessons on specific sound/letter combinations will help students apply phonetic understanding to spelling, reading, or writing. In the example of Figure 2.1, the teacher can use the poster or chart temporarily or continue to leave it up as part of a word wall.

FIGURE 2.1	PRONUNCIATION CHART	PARTS OF THE BODY
Phonic generaliza-tion chart.	Single vowels between two consonants are usually short. ⟷	Capillaries (<u>cap</u> il <u>lar</u> ies) Gullet (<u>gul</u> <u>let</u>)
	Single vowels at the beginning of a syllable are generally short. ⟷	Intestine (<u>in</u> tes tine)
	Single vowels at the end of a syllable are usually long. ⟷	Bronchi (bron <u>chi</u>)
	Single vowels followed by a consonant, then a silent *e,* are long. ⟷	Platelets (<u>plate</u> lets)
	Consonant digraph (ph /f/, ck /k/, gm /m/) ⟷	Esophagus (e so<u>ph</u> a gus) Diaphragm (di a <u>phragm</u>)

LABELING

PRIMARY
INTERMEDIATE
ESL

Placing labels on things in the classroom develops students' phonic, decoding, and spelling strategies. They use the visual clue of the item, such as a door, match it with the label, then practice saying and reading it. Labeling supports writing in the classroom, as well as reading, by providing learners with a reference to help them in spelling. If teachers introduce writing using the labels or a word wall by talking about the sounds the letters make as students write them, they are reinforcing strong phonics word recognition skills.

SHARING READING

PRIMARY
ESL

Writing stories, talking about language, and reading together support the oral-to-written connections for emerging literacy. Songs, rhymes, word games, chart poems, tongue twisters (alliteration patterns), and chants all draw attention to sounds and connect sounds to letters and words. Encouraging children to tell or share what they know about a text based on the letters, sounds, and pictures during these oral experiences assists students in learning from each other and helps the teacher identify individual awareness. First, teachers preview a text with the students and begin reading. As they come in contact with words that are new to the students, teachers can use phonics by modeling the sounding-out process to read the word. Sharing the story, looking at words, modeling word recognition strategies, and discussing the meaning of the book all encourage reading skills.

VARIATION. Thinking aloud or sharing during reading is also helpful for older students. Suppose Mr. Aaron was reading *Harry Potter and the Goblet of Fire* to his seventh graders and came across a word, "parseltongue," which his students would not know. Taking a teachable moment, he wrote the word letter by letter while sounding out each letter and then chunking them into syllables to pronounce the word. He also made use of structural analysis, which is discussed in the next section. Later, when the class was studying their science lesson, they used their decoding skills again to figure out "photosynthesis" picking out some word parts like "photo" and "the" and applying phonics generalizations to "syn" (short vowel in CVC pattern) and again in "sis." By putting the sounds together the class figured out the word.

INTERMEDIATE
MIDDLE

MATCHING AND SORTING

Connecting sounds to letters/words and letters/words to sounds helps students process phonemic awareness and decoding skills. For example: Sort the /c/ initial sounds from this list of foods: carrot, cabbage, apple, cake, banana, cookie, orange. Another example is to have the children match the beginning sound in socks, pants, blouse, and shirt with shoes, blanket, parrot, and sun.

PRIMARY
INTERMEDIATE

VARIATION. Sorting by the number of syllables may be helpful for older students who have difficulty sounding out polysyllabic words, such as: say•ing, e•man•ci•pa•tion, proc•la•ma•tion, pres•i•dent, and Feb•ru•ary.

MIDDLE
SECONDARY

DICTIONARY USE

Learning how to use the pronunciation key in the dictionary entry will help independent readers decode unfamiliar written words, often linking the words to the students' listening vocabulary. This is a valuable strategy for students that should be taught, and teachers may take advantage of teachable moments for reinforcing the phonics connection as well. For example, if a student is reading the word "catastrophe" and asks the teacher how to pronounce it, the teacher might say, "Let's look it up together and see how to say it." Cunningham (as cited in Robinson, McKenna, & Wedman, 1996) found that having struggling readers find polysyllabic words in the dictionary and pronounce them added greatly to their word recognition ease in reading. See pages 69 and 119 for more information about teaching students to use the dictionary pronunciation key.

ALL

WHAT STRATEGIES CAN STUDENTS USE TO REINFORCE PHONICS?

WORD BANKS

ALL

Students collect words that begin with each of the sounds to collect in their own word banks or word collections. The words can be written on note cards and kept in a file box, or the words can be compiled in a list and kept in a notebook. Students then are encouraged to refer to these cards or lists for future writing activities. Some students become word collectors and enjoy finding new words, sounding them out and discovering what they mean. Making a collection of new words is not just an activity for young readers; it is great for older readers as they encounter more and more difficult texts with specific technical vocabulary in the content areas.

INVENTED OR DEVELOPMENTAL SPELLING

PRIMARY
INTERMEDIATE
ESL

Reinforcing students' phonic awareness by allowing **invented or developmental spelling** can be a powerful tool in enabling students to write. Developmental spelling allows students to tap into their broader, more sophisticated listening vocabulary when composing text rather than be limited to the words they know how to spell. Before asking for help, students can practice spelling unfamiliar words while writing. Students at all ages should be encouraged to have a go at spelling or writing words using the sound/letter relationships.

When describing the purple monster he colored to illustrate his story for the second grade open house Matt wrote "prpl monstr." Erin, a fifth grader, wrote, "Uranius and Saturn are two planets within our solar system" in her listening guide, from a video her teacher had played. Both students used phonics clues to help them write and later read.

SAYING WORDS SLOWLY, BECOMING AWARE OF SOUNDS

PRIMARY

Listening for the sounds in the words will help students decode words during reading or predict the spelling of words in writing. Sliding a marker or finger from left to right will help them identify the sounds. Practice in building rhymes and finding unknown words in the dictionary, then trying to pronounce them, can build decoding skills.

MIDDLE
SECONDARY

VARIATION. For older students, the concept of stretching out words might be particularly helpful in sounding out polysyllabic words such as Pythagorean theorem and hypotenuse.

LINKING SOUNDS TOGETHER

ALL

Blending sounds in patterns that are identifiable will help readers and writers respond more quickly to text. For example: Knowing that "tion" is pronounced /shun/ as in "station" will help a reader decode other words. An example for elementary grades is "motion" or "location." The same "tion" example would be "transition" or "retribution" at a middle or secondary level.

ASSESSMENT: HOW IS PHONICS ASSESSED?

Assessing phonics awareness and phonics use should take place before, during, and after reading and writing, preferably in authentic activities. The best evidence of how students are applying phonics as a word recognition skill is to listen to them read and to look at their writing. As students read and decode words they struggle with or as they write and sound out spellings of challenging words, teachers can glimpse how this strategy assists their students.

Informal Assessment Activities

Listening to children is a principal approach in assessing students' use of phonemic awareness and phonics skills (Griffith & Olsen, 1992). Checklists and anecdotal records can aid teachers in documenting students' progress. Assessment can take place during games such as "rhyming words" and "name that sound" ("What sound is found at the end of cook?") as a teacher listens carefully to the answers children give.

Informal observations often reveal as much as formal assessment when teachers are cognizant of the decisions their readers are making. For instance, while three first graders were singing the name song ("Hanna, Hanna, bo banna, banana, fanna fo fanna, fe fi mo, manna, Hanna"), the teacher could easily identify that these children were able to rhyme, make onset substitutions, and follow a pattern. Although this would not be considered a formal assessment of their phonics knowledge, it did indicate to the teacher some strong skills the students were using. Another example is to use a checklist for phonic generalizations to accompany a student's sample oral reading. The checklist might look like the following:

Correctly Used	Incorrectly Used	Not Observed	Phonics Skill
			[Student . . .] identified initial sound in decoding, looked for familiar word parts, sounded out word by letters

Another example of an informal assessment activity is to have students take a high-interest or well-known word and substitute the initial sound using every letter of the alphabet. For example, using Bruce Degan's *Jamberry,* students would say "jamberry, amberry, bamberry, camberry," and so on. Teachers also could have students replace the middle sounds with all of the vowel sounds ("bat" changes to "bet, bit, bot, but").

Informal Reading Inventory

Most informal reading inventories (described in Unit 1) have word lists for determining students' sight word levels. IRI's also provide an excellent opportunity for teachers to assess readers' decoding process. How readers pronounce the word or attempt to say it informs the teacher how the students are using initial sounds. Similarly, during the oral reading component of an IRI, teachers can uncover breakdowns in decoding and identify appropriate application of phonics skills.

Formal Testing

Some assessment for phonics applications may be done in a standardized test format required by a school system. Types of information gathered from these assessments include successful identification of initial, middle, or ending sounds, identification of word parts or **affixes**, and ability to spell.

An example of a formal test for phonemic awareness might be an initial consonant sound test. In various published tests, teachers pose several pictures for a student to flip through, say the name of the picture, and give the initial sound they hear in the word, as illustrated.

lion /l/   horse /h/   turtle /t/

The teacher could see and hear that this student was able to distinguish initial consonant sounds for l, h, and t. Another example is to have students sort pictures by initial sounds to provide assessment data.

Evaluating Writing

One of the most effective ways to assess students' knowledge of phonics skills is to analyze their writing. Teachers can see how students match letters to the sounds they hear in words. If an emergent writer spells the word "happy" as "hape," the teacher knows that the student can hear the sounds and is attempting to match those sounds with the letters he or she knows makes those sounds. Students who are using this type of sound spelling are using their knowledge of phonics to spell.

The same is true at the secondary level. Teachers can glean insight into the phonics skills that students are using during their writing. An example is the student's writing "chorafill" for "chlorophyll" in a science lab report.

2.2 Structural Analysis: What Are Its Parts?

WHAT IS STRUCTURAL ANALYSIS?

Structural analysis is the means by which words can be recognized by their word parts or meaning units. Structural analysis generally entails looking at roots (base or main parts of words), prefixes (word parts placed before root parts of words), and suffixes (word parts placed after root parts), as well as syllabication (the division of words into sounds). As mentioned in Unit 1, structural analysis is one of three word recognition skills identified by a number of reading authorities for many years. The other two are phonics analysis and contextual analysis, with configuration clues, picture clues, sight word knowledge, and dictionary usage as additional skills. Structural analysis could be considered the internal clues available concerning words—the roots and affixes (both prefixes and suffixes) found within words.

Although reading authorities have used the term *structural analysis* over time, classroom teachers usually do not use the term in communicating with students. At the primary level, instruction involving structural analysis typically uses simpler terminology and the specific element being studied, such as *word families, word beginnings,* and *word endings.* At the middle school and secondary levels, instruction involving structural analysis might be referred to as *word study, Latin or Greek word study,* or similar terms. At the university level, instruction involving structural analysis is often referred to as the study of medical terminology, scientific terminology, or other specific areas.

In the study of linguistics, a different and more precise scientific terminology is used to describe the type of word recognition skills that reading authorities sometimes call structural analysis. Linguists use the term *morphemic analysis,* in which words are analyzed in terms of **morphemes**, the smallest meaning unit in a word. Free morphemes are words that can stand alone as word meaning units and cannot be broken into smaller units of meaning. Bound morphemes are word parts that must be attached to free morphemes to have meaning. Linguists, speech therapists, and similar professionals use precise terminology—here defined quite simply and generally in parentheses—such as morphemes (meaning units), graphemes (written letter units), phonemes (sound units), and **grapho-phonemics** (the study of the relationship between written language or orthography and spoken language or phonology). Many classroom teachers tend to use simpler language when working with students, as the precision required by the profession is not necessary here.

By whatever label, the ability to use structural analysis is important to readers. By studying word roots and affixes, students are able to learn many groups of words quickly and to determine the meaning of new words from knowing their roots and affixes. Affixes are sometimes taught as part of syllabication. Affixes include prefixes (e.g., mis, un, bi, in, un, tri) and suffixes (e.g., ing, er, ed, ly). Affixes may change the meaning of the word, as in "trial" (event) and "pretrial" (leading up to the trial), or they may change the function, as in "play" (present tense) and "played" (past tense). The next section covers affixes in more detail.

HOW IS STRUCTURAL ANALYSIS TAUGHT?

Structural analysis is particularly helpful to students beyond the beginning reading acquisition level. After primary grade levels, reading vocabulary and terminology becomes increasingly complex and scientific. Structural analysis enables readers to learn many words and word meanings by focusing on frequently used roots and affixes. Scientific and professional words in English often come from Latin and Greek. Appendix B lists common Latin and Greek word roots. Readers who study word roots or parts (more formally called *cognates*) make quick strides in adding sets of words to their reading, writing, speaking, and listening vocabularies.

Root words. A **root** is the part of a word that carries its main meaning. By identifying what part of a word is the root word, students can figure out unknown words. For example, in looking at the word "rejection," students can find the root "ject," which means to throw or hurl, and use this knowledge to guess that "rejection" has something to do with throwing. They could use their knowledge of the prefix "re," meaning back or again, and the suffix "ion," meaning the act or condition of, to surmise that "rejection" has to do with the act of throwing back.

Prefixes. **Prefixes** are word parts that are added to the beginning of a root or word. By teaching students the meaning of the most commonly used prefixes, teachers are giving students an invaluable tool to figure out unknown words. For example, the prefix "tri" in "triangle" informs the reader of *three* angles. Appendix C lists common prefixes with definitions and examples.

Suffixes. **Suffixes** are word parts at the end of a root or word. For example, in the word "equitable," the root "equi" means equal and the suffix "able" means able to. Therefore, using the knowledge of the root word and suffix, students can figure out that the word means "able to be equal." Using this knowledge, students have broken down a seemingly difficult word and made it easy. Another example, adding the suffix "ful," meaning full of, to the word "help" gives the reader the understanding that someone who is "helpful" is full of help. Appendix D lists common suffixes with definitions and examples.

Syllables. Words are made up of **syllables.** Each syllable is a unit of sound, and each word must have at least one syllable. Each syllable has one vowel sound—a sound made by pushing air through open lips. Syllables often are identified as being open or closed. An *open syllable* that ends with a vowel usually has a long vowel sound (it says its own name) as in /ta/ in table (tá•ble). A *closed syllable,* which ends with a consonant, such as "tab" and "let," in the word "tablet" (tab•let) usually has a short vowel sound (with the short "a" sound as in the beginning sound of "apple").

One effective way to help students identify the different syllables in a word is to have them place their hand on their chin and then say a word with more than one syllable. The chin will move with each syllable. Once they understand the concept, students can clap with each syllable. Teaching students to recognize syllables in a word gives them a means to separate parts of the word into more manageable units.

Compound words. A **compound word** is made up of two complete words put together to form a new word. Examples of compound words are "doghouse," "boyfriend," and "football." When readers are unsure of a word's meaning, one strategy they can use is to break the word apart and look at the meanings of each individual word. For example in "doghouse," the two words combined means it is a house for a dog. Sometimes, however, compound words cannot be taken literally. For instance, "butterfly" does not mean that butter can fly!

Structural analysis is a process that teachers use both incidentally and directly at all levels of instruction, particularly beyond students' first two years of school. Teachers who apply structural analysis *incidentally* take advantage of teachable moments by regularly taking apart new or reintroduced words, by asking students to identify the roots, prefixes, and suffixes and connecting them with other known words containing the same root words. Teachers who use structural analysis *directly* build in regular instructional time to help students systematically build their knowledge of word roots and affixes.

Incidental teaching of structural analysis might be undertaken routinely by asking students to take apart words to figure out the meaning from root words and affixes as these words arise within units of content study. In a second-grade class the teacher introduced a new vocabulary word—chickens—to the students. The teacher began by having the students look at the root word "chick" and add the "en" ending relating back to their decoding practice. Then the teacher asked the children, "What happens to 'chicken' when I add the 's'"? The children responded, "It means there are a whole bunch of chickens." The teacher asked the class to make a rule to put on the writing chart—*Things to Remember in Writing*. The children decided on:

Use s to change words to mean more than one.

Next the teacher asked the students to apply the new rule to another word, "playhouse." First they broke down the word into "play" and "house." Structural analysis of this word revealed that it was made up of two other words, and the class talked about compound words. Finally the teacher asked if anyone could tell the class how to change the word to mean more than one playhouse (referring back to the new writing rule). They all responded with "playhouses."

At the middle or secondary school level, a teacher might use structural analysis in considering more thoroughly the word "comprehension" as the class prepares to work on reading comprehension. He could ask class members to guess the root part within the term "comprehend." After someone has identified "prehend," the teacher could ask them to name any other words that use "prehend" or "prehender" as he jots the terms on the chalkboard. The teacher then might model to the class his actions as he apprehends a criminal, demonstrating the action of seizing or grasping. Students might be reinforced in "grasping" the meaning of "prehend" by discussing prehensile tails or long prehensile fingernails. Through such incidental teaching on the part of the teacher using structural analysis, students could develop the practice of using structural analysis themselves to recognize words that are not yet sight words and to unlock the meanings of new words.

In addition, a teacher can use direct instruction of structural analysis to help students build stronger word recognition and vocabulary. For instance, students will benefit from studying commonly used Latin and Greek roots (see Appendix B), such as "astr" or star, "logos" or study, "decca" or ten. Students can learn these roots and affixes from direct and systematic teaching—individually, in groupings, in categories—or by whatever means teachers or students devise. Students can learn new words by associating the root words with a known word. For instance, if students know that an astronaut is someone who works in space and they know that "astr" means star, this may help them figure out the meaning of "astrology."

Students at all levels can develop structural analysis notebooks, dictionaries, or word banks, either through teachers' direct instruction or through their own initiative. By learning some commonly used word roots, students can learn many new words with relative ease, particularly words that come from scientific terminology. Other possible direct instruction models appropriate for various grade levels are included among the strategies presented next.

WHAT STRATEGIES CAN TEACHERS USE TO REINFORCE STRUCTURAL ANALYSIS?

One principle that reading authorities often suggest, supported by recent interpretations of brain-based learning, is that students learn more completely when their learning is active and hands-on and they enjoy their learning. All of the activities for reinforcing structural analysis that follow engage students actively.

ROOT CHAIN

SECONDARY

A root chain begins with a word containing a common word root, and students build upon it in a chain fashion (Glazier, 1993).

1. List a word at the top of the chalkboard.
2. Select a part of the word that can be added to another word part to build a second word.
3. Select a different part of the second word and add a different word part to form a third.
4. Continue this process until a predetermined number of words has been formed, as shown in the following example.

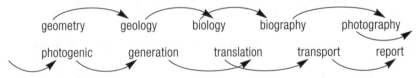

geometry → geology → biology → biography → photography

photogenic → generation → translation → transport → report

SPELLING

ALL

A good time to reinforce the structure of words is when introducing spelling words. The first time words are introduced, teachers can break apart each word and show students how the word was formed, what each part means, and how the parts work together to form a new word. This helps students understand the word and also helps them learn how to spell the word. For example, "rejection" broken apart is "re" (meaning again), "ject" (meaning toss or hurl), and "ion" (meaning condition of or state). Putting it together, "rejection" is the state of being tossed aside again.

CONCENTRATION

INTERMEDIATE
MIDDLE

This common word game works particularly well for strengthening structural analysis.

1. Write the same word on each of two note cards.

2. Develop several pairs using the directions in step 1.

3. To play the game, mix the cards and place the stack face down on the table or floor.

4. Have the first player turn over two word cards.

5. For strengthening structural analysis, a player who turns over two word cards with the same word has to be able to pronounce the words correctly, say the word root, and give the root part's meaning. If the player answers correctly, he or she takes the cards. If he or she answers incorrectly, the word cards are turned over again in the same position.

6. Have the next player take a turn.

7. Continue the game either for a given time or until all cards are uncovered and claimed. The winner is the player with the most word cards at the end of the game.

If intended to reinforce strictly structural analysis, all words used should contain word roots. The number of sets laid down depends upon the age and ability of students and the time available. In the example below, the student would say: "Unfold. 'Fold' is the word root and 'un' is the prefix meaning 'undo,' so 'unfold' means to 'take out the folds.'"

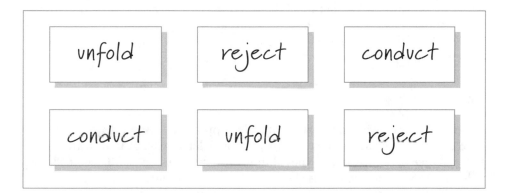

VARIATION. As a second check at the end of the game, the winner might be asked to again pronounce the words correctly, identify their roots and give their meanings. Students usually look forward to playing Concentration, and it works well as a closing activity for the day.

INTERMEDIATE
MIDDLE

VARIATION. A modification for primary-age children might be to change meaning by using just suffixes: horses, dogs, cats, picked, helped, jumped, running, walking, hopping. A follow-up activity might be to sort words into categories by root parts, as in *animals* and *actions* for the words suggested above.

PRIMARY

MODIFIED CLOZE ACTIVITY

The cloze procedure described in Unit 1 can be adapted in a **modified cloze activity** to provide a classroom structural analysis activity. In developing structural analysis, the teacher may delete words that include root words from the passage. In this case, students typically are given a copy of a text in which every

INTERMEDIATE
MIDDLE
SECONDARY

deleted word contains a root word. Students are to fill in the blanks with words that make sense based on their overall understanding of the text. A sample cloze is included in the assessment section in Unit 1. To prepare a modified cloze activity focusing on structural analysis:

1. Choose a short text that is relatively easy for the students to read.
2. In typing the text, insert a blank line of identical length (11 blanks is a recommended length for all lines) for every chosen word that has a root or affix.
3. Place root words (and possibly several choices of words containing word roots) at the bottom of the cloze passage. For instance, if the deleted word is "thermometer," the root words and words at the bottom of the sheet might include "thermo, thermos, thermometer, thermal, metric, meter, and metronome."
4. Have students read the text and fill in each blank with the word they think makes sense.

MATCHING CLOZE EXERCISE

INTERMEDIATE
MIDDLE
SECONDARY

This activity is identical to the cloze activity described above except that students are given a random listing of the deleted words at the top or bottom of the page. Students can check off the words in the list as they use them to fill in the blanks. As with the regular cloze exercise, this activity helps students practice structural analysis.

MAZE PROCEDURE

INTERMEDIATE
MIDDLE
SECONDARY

The **maze procedure** is a variation of a cloze procedure. As in the cloze, a passage of text is selected and every *n*th word is deleted, except that in the maze, three choices are provided as possibilities for the missing word (see example below). Only one of the words should make sense. For strengthening structural analysis, the incorrect or distracter words may use other word roots. Because this form of the cloze provides students with three word choices to fill in the blank, this activity might be helpful to use the first time teachers introduce a cloze activity or to use with students who need to strengthen their ability to use structural analysis. Using the maze to help students work on structural analysis, for example, the choice words can be similar except for affixes, as in this sample:

undetermined

The boy knew where the fair was because it was in a(n) <u>predetermined</u> place.

indeterminate

AFFIX GAME

PRIMARY
INTERMEDIATE
MIDDLE
ESL

This activity reinforces the use of affixes.

1. Divide the class into groups of three or four.
2. Say a common prefix or suffix such as "un," "pre," "able," or "less."

3. Give the groups 1 minute to write as many words as they can think of with that affix.

4. Have the groups count the number of words they came up with.

5. Starting with the group that has the most words, have each group read its list.

6. Have the other groups and the teacher serve as the judges to eliminate any words that are not real words.

WORD PART GAME

Playing the word part game can help students practice structural analysis.

PRIMARY
INTERMEDIATE
MIDDLE
ESL

1. Make cards with a root or root word, a prefix, or a suffix on each card. (Cards can be laminated for durability.)

2. Pass out the cards so each student has one card. Have students carry a piece of paper with them to write down the new word they are able to make.

3. Upon the teacher's signal, have students stand up and mingle with each other, looking for students with cards they can match with their own card to make a new word. They write on their piece of paper each word they are able to make.

4. Have the students continue to move around the room making new words with their classmates.

5. After a predetermined length of time, stop the activity with a signal and have the students count their words.

6. Starting with the student who has the most words, ask the students to read their lists.

WHAT STRATEGIES CAN STUDENTS USE TO REINFORCE STRUCTURAL ANALYSIS?

APPLYING CLAY'S 5-FINGER SUGGESTION

Clay suggests using a **5-finger strategy** to attack unknown words:

PRIMARY
INTERMEDIATE
MIDDLE
ESL

1. Look at the picture and think about the story.
2. Reread the sentence and get your mouth ready.
3. Does it sound right? Can I say it that way?
4. Read on to see if that will help me.
5. Do I see a part that I know in the word?

The fifth and final element in Clay's suggestion encourages the use of structural analysis. Clay's set of suggestions builds in looking at word roots as well as smaller words within a word. The 5-finger suggestion provides students with a specific strategy they can use when they come to a word they do not know. Teachers can make a poster or bulletin board with these steps for students to refer to when they are reading on their own. When first introducing this strategy, teachers can model it and work through the steps with the students.

WORD BANKS

ALL

Students can collect in their own word banks or word collections words that use certain roots or root words and affixes. They can write the words on note cards and keep them in a file box, or compile them in a list and keep it in a notebook. Students are encouraged to refer to these cards/lists for future writing activities. If kept in a file box, the words can be alphabetized by the root (example: astr—astronaut, astronomer, astronomy, astrology).

WORD WALLS

ALL

When emphasizing structural analysis, some word walls can be organized by the roots or root words and affixes that students are learning. When a class is introduced to a new root, students can write it on a slip of paper and add it to the wall. The roots or affixes can be arranged alphabetically on the wall, with room to add new sets of roots and affixes. For instance, under the root "graph," students may place autograph, photograph, telegraph, and graphic.

READING RODS

PRIMARY
INTERMEDIATE
ESL

Reading rods are an active manipulative for reinforcing structural analysis. The teacher can make reading rods as follows.

1. Select a dowel rod or broom or mop handle approximately 12–14 inches long.
2. Develop a stack of cards (note cards) with different roots printed on each card.
3. Develop a stack of cards for various prefixes and a stack for suffixes.
4. Punch two holes at the top of each card in each stack and connect the cards with notebook rings or shower rings.
5. Slide these rings over the dowel so the order is prefixes, roots, then suffixes.
6. Ask students to flip the cards in various combinations to make new words.

Most often, words are termed using only two of the three stacks—for example, using only prefixes and roots or roots and suffixes. The prefix card might be "tele" with a matching root of "phone," with students flipping to alternate the root parts "graph," "gram," and "cable" to make the words telephone, telegraph, telegram, and telecable. Manipulatives, such as reading rods, allow students to see the word elements separately, and these are particularly helpful to students who have difficulty conceptualizing combining word parts.

ASSESSMENT: HOW IS STRUCTURAL ANALYSIS ASSESSED?

Informal Reading Inventory

The teacher can informally determine whether students are able to use structural analysis by listening to students read passages aloud during an IRI (described in Unit I). After having the student read aloud a passage and complete the comprehension section, the teacher could go back to a word with a root element that the student had difficulty decoding and ask the student to look for the root within the word. The teacher could ask if the student knows other words that have that part, and what that root would likely mean. The teacher also could take note of the word and prepare a mini-lesson for the class later, asking about that root, other words, and their probable meanings.

Running Record

A running record, as explained in Unit I, is an individually administered reading assessment that necessitates only the child's copy of the printed text and a sheet of paper. Structural analysis can be evaluated by looking at students' ability or inability to decode words with roots and affixes. This evaluation would likely take place after the student has completed the running record. While Miss Kate was taking a running record of John's oral reading, she recorded that he had substituted "circled" for "circus." John's structural analysis broke down at the word ending part.

Checklist

Teachers can use a checklist of students' knowledge of roots and affixes or include such a section within a larger checklist of word recognition skills. Using a checklist for structural analysis may look like the sample in Figure 2.2, in which dates are recorded.

SKILL	INTRODUCED	IN PROGRESS	MASTERED
Uses *un* to mean *not*	8/16	9/23	10/20
Applies (s) or (es) for plurals	8/22	9/14	
Identified syllable in polysyllabic words	5/9		

FIGURE 2.2

Sample checklist for roots and affixes.

2.3 Context Clues: Does It Make Sense? Does It Sound Right?

Context clues, sometimes called contextual analysis, become important as readers encounter more difficult print and as their reading ability matures. For example, using the "sense of the sentence," the reader discovers whether the word "read" is, "I will *read* the book tonight "or "Yesterday, I *read* the newspaper." The skillful reader also can derive the meaning of unknown words by making educated guesses about what words mean from how they are used in context. Readers seem to be able to use context clues best to unlock words when the material they are reading is not at their frustration level. Harris and Sipay (1990) summarize several researchers' findings by saying, "The word recognition of poor readers is facilitated by context when the content of the text is within the pupils' conceptual grasp and when the name of unknown words does not exceed their word-recognition ability" (p. 447).

Emphasizing development of context clues is important because it makes struggling readers more aware that reading has to make sense. Older readers who lack well-developed reading skills seem not to self-correct as they make miscues that do not make sense. Because they tend to read only when required to do so and have spent years seeing text not make sense, they are used to continuing regardless of whether the text has meaning to them. Context clues help the reader to use the sense of the sentence to recognize words and meanings, and their use places a needed focus on text comprehension.

Context clues help readers look for meaning. An example of the importance of search for meaning is illustrated in "Jabberwocky," from Lewis Carroll's *Alice in Wonderland.* The poem has remained deservedly famous, in part for the pleasure that readers derive from being able to bring sense and meaning into the seemingly nonsensical cadence of the poem: "Twas Brillig and the Slithy Toab did gire and gimble in the wabe." Readers know Brillig and the Slithy Toab are "things" or nouns; that "gire" and "gimble" are action words or verbs; and that the "giring" and "gimbling" took place in the "wabe," which seems to be the location of a noun. While having fun with this and similar nonsense poems, readers are able to derive approximate meanings of the poem from context clues—both semantics (word meaning knowledge and a sense of the text's meaning) and syntax (word order and the uses of words).

SEMANTICS: DOES IT MAKE SENSE?

Semantics is one of the main cueing systems researchers indicate good readers use to identify words (Clay, 1991; Goodman, 1986; Pinnell & Fountas, 1998; Routman, 1991). Semantics can be defined as "the meaning of words." Harris and Sipay (1990) state, "Semantic cues involve word-meaning knowledge and a general sense of the text's meaning" (p. 448). Often when we think about semantic cues, we look at how readers comprehend a whole sentence or paragraph, but semantics also may be closely related to vocabulary and prior knowledge.

Most young children have a verbal, working knowledge and understanding of the language used in their homes. They understand the way their family communicates and are able to understand most of what is said to them. They understand what makes sense when language is used. This, then, is the basis of semantics: Does it make sense?

For language to be useful, however, it must make sense within the context of the whole conversation or text. The concept of **semantic cues** cannot be discussed without understanding that semantics looks at the relationship and is dependent upon the surrounding text. Teaching semantic cues would not be helpful using an isolated list of words as text. Goodman (1986) suggests that "readers construct meaning during reading. They use their prior learning and experience to make sense of text [as they are reading]" (p. 38). By using their background knowledge, readers may make sense of unknown words in the text selection by reading the known words, phrases, and sentences in the surrounding text. This stresses the theoretical view of top-down processing of comprehension. Top-down text processing, according to Harris and Hodges (1995), is "reading comprehension that begins with and is controlled by the experiences and expectations that the reader brings to the text" (p. 256). Semantic cues are clues to comprehension that assist readers in making meaning based on other words and inferences in the surrounding text.

SYNTACTIC CUES: DOES IT SOUND RIGHT?

Syntax has been defined by Harris and Hodges (1995) as "the study of how sentences are formed and of the grammatical rules that govern their formation" (p. 249). Syntactic cues have to do with the grammatical structure of a sentence or the placement of words in a sentence or phrase. Children learn syntax through language. For example, if you were to say to a 3-year-old, "Pick up your _____," the child most likely would fill in the blank with a noun such as "toys," "clothes," or "books." The child is using syntactic cues to fill in the blank. Although 3-year-olds probably have no idea what a noun is, they know what "sounds right" because of their knowledge of the language.

Children learn through their interactions with others and language what kinds of words make sense. For example, when Kevin read the sentence, "The water changes into steam" from the book *All About Electricity* by Melvin Berger, instead of reading "steam," he said "smoke." Even though he read the word incorrectly, he was using his knowledge of syntax to replace a noun with a noun.

Knowledge of syntax can give readers their first cue as to what type of word an unknown word will be. Syntactic cues include parts of speech, plurals, spelling, and word order. One of the best ways by which students learn syntax is their experience with language. Students need opportunities to interact with others in the classroom. As they read, write, listen, and speak, they continually are learning more and developing their awareness of language and its uses. Through these interactions, students learn what words sound right as they read.

Teachers can reinforce syntactic cues by talking about what types of words make sense in certain places in the sentence. Teaching parts of speech (noun, pronoun, verb, adverb, adjective) may take place during the regular language arts instruction time or may be integrated in the reading class. As they teach about syntactic cues, teachers may capitalize on students' understanding or experience with parts of speech. As students are reading and making miscues, teachers can talk about what types of words would make sense.

For example, Kara was reading recreationally when she came across the word "condominium" in *The View from Saturday*, by E. L. Konigsburg. The sentence she stumbled in reading was, "He lives in a high-rise condominium on the beach in Florida" (p. 25). Kara figured out that the big word had to be some kind of building (noun) because she knew the person lived there and she knew what high-rise meant. Then she decoded the "condo" word part and "condominium" sprang to her mind because her grandmother lives in one. Kara used context clues as her first word recognition strategy in this case and then turned to some additional strategies to help herself read the text.

HOW ARE CONTEXT CLUES TAUGHT?

When helping students learn how to use context clues, teachers use both semantic cues and syntactic cues. Because semantic cues and syntactic cues are so closely interrelated, to teach one in isolation without mentioning the other is difficult. The connection between the cueing systems calls for learning word recognition strategies and skills in real reading experiences, not in isolation.

Teachers and parents alike can help strengthen children's use of context clues by verbally communicating with children. This exposes children to language and the communicative value of using it effectively. Talking with children expands their background knowledge of topics and vocabulary. Vocabulary thus plays an important part in the overall meaning of a given text and what the reader will understand. Readers who have a strong vocabulary can tap into the context or meaning of a text to help them recognize unknown words. Teachers facilitate students' learning of vocabulary and the building of experiential knowledge by encouraging talk at home and fostering talk in the classroom. (See pages 55–61 for a further discussion of vocabulary development.)

Teachers should discuss with parents the importance of talking with children in the home about a variety of topics and encourage parents to become active in the language and vocabulary acquisition process. This can be done at parent–teacher conferences or by sending home discussion-oriented "homework" questions. Classroom discussions and a variety of talk opportunities during the school day will add and support comprehension based on context.

As discussed previously, semantic cueing may be described as using the surrounding words and meaning to figure out an unknown word. When readers are faced with an unfamiliar word, they use semantic cueing if they continue by skipping the word while still comprehending the text. Then as they return to the unknown word, they recognize the word through the meaning, supported by other clues such as beginning letter sounds.

Textbook publishers make use of semantic cues when they italicize important words. This can signal readers that the surrounding text contains the definition of the unknown word. Teachers can point out this strategy to children as they read passages together. Teachers also can give readers practice in figuring out words through the use of semantic cueing by using trade books and other reading materials in which the teacher highlights key vocabulary.

A fun activity for children to practice using semantic cues is to give them a text with some teacher-identified words and have the students highlight or underline the parts of the text that helped them figure out the unfamiliar word. For example, Ms. Weatherly gave her students a text containing the sentence: "Sally felt vulnerable as she walked alone down the shadow-filled forest path listening to the howling wind blow through the thick trees unsure of where she was going." Her students struggled over the word "vulnerable." She asked them to read the sentence again, looking at the other words in the sentence. Then the teacher asked the students what they might predict the word "vulnerable" to mean. Suggestions were "scared, nervous, uneasy, and unsure." After praising the predictions, Ms. Weatherly drew their attention once more to the clues "alone" and "unsure." Sam said it made him think Sally was scared that something was going to happen. The class agreed that the clues "alone," "unsure," "shadow-filled," and "howling" all helped to define vulnerable as "susceptible to physical injury" (*Webster's II New College Dictionary*).

Supporting this process of using context clues to uncover the meaning and then the words, teachers can model a strategy called **think-alouds,** a strategy in which a teacher states aloud his or her thinking processes (Davey, 1983). Through think-alouds, teachers are able to show students their own thought processes so the children know how syntactic cues support reading and help with word recognition. When teachers are reading aloud and come to a word they do not know (or pretend they don't know), they can stop and talk about what type of word would make sense.

Suppose a teacher is reading aloud to students as they are following along. The teacher can pause at a word, describe the feeling of not knowing the word, and decide to read on. Upon reaching the end of the selection, the teacher can direct the class's attention back to the unfamiliar word and use the meaning of the text to figure out that missing word. For example, after reading the sentence, "Because Dan's family was not very demonstrative, he wasn't used to being hugged," the teacher might stop and say:

> "*Demonstrative* is not a word we hear very often. When I come to a word I don't know, I look at the other words in the sentence to see if they give me any clues as to what the word might mean. The sentence states that Dan is not used to being hugged, so maybe Dan is not used to people showing him how they feel about him. So 'demonstrative' in this sentence probably means showing or demonstrating affection. Now let's look it up in the dictionary to see if we are right."

The teacher has modeled a think-aloud for how to figure out an unknown word using semantic cueing.

Mrs. Wilson wrote the following morning message on the chart paper:

Today we will be going on a field trip to the observatory. We will leave about 12:00. We will see some interesting sights such as planets and stars.

While writing the sentence, Mrs. Wilson began a think-aloud to illustrate her use of syntactic cues.

> "Today we will be going on a field trip to the—hummmm . . . what is that word? It must be a place that we are going to visit. I guess I will keep on reading and try to figure out where we are going. We will leave about 12:00. 'Twelve o'clock' means we will leave just after lunch. We will see some interesting sights such as planets and stars. Oh, that's what that 'o' word must be—'observatory'."

Teachers also can teach context clues when readers encounter word substitutions in text. When students come across a word they do not recognize and substitute a word that seems to make sense temporarily or permanently, they have successfully applied context clues. The teachable moment lends itself to indirectly making immediate connections for the students. Sometimes the substitutions are based on synonyms within selected pieces of text. For example, when John read the book, *When I Grow Up,* by Mercer Mayer, he read "I will be a policeman and help everyone cross the street" instead of the exact wording, "I will be a police officer and help everybody cross the street." He substituted "policeman" for "police officer" and "everyone" for "everybody." His teacher could use this example to show the class how John was using his own vocabulary to help him figure out the words.

Another way in which teachers may help readers make the connection to context clues is to reinforce "graphic similarity" (Wilde, 1997, p. 128). This type of connection involves substituting words that look alike, such as "house" and "home." If the substituted word resembles another word and still makes sense, the reader has used another form of semantic understanding to help comprehension. For instance, in the sentence, "Susie was the most energetic cheerleader on the squad," a reader might substitute "active" using a synonym, or "enthusiastic" using graphic similarity. In either case, substitution works for meaning and helps readers identify the unknown word.

In a direct teaching model, a **minilesson** is one alternative to teaching about context clues. The steps in a minilesson may include calling attention to a skill or strategy, giving guided practice, providing independent practice, and finally checking for appropriate use or comprehension. The teacher may want to build in opportunities to teach readers how to use the semantic cueing system to ensure that they are applying the strategies when needed.

Minilesson for teaching about context clues

Mrs. Hoskins used the book *Swimmy,* by Leo Lionni, to teach a minilesson.

1. Introduction of the skill.   Mrs. Hoskins introduced context clues as a word recognition skill. She shared with her class that sometimes readers can figure out what a new word is if they listen to what the author is talking about.

2. Guided practice.   Mrs. Hoskins instructed the student to listen carefully and help her fill in the blank in the story about a friendly fish named Swimmy. "[Swimmy] taught them to swim close together, each in his own place, and when they had learned to swim like one ____ fish, he said, 'I'll be the eye.'"

In this minilesson, the teacher skipped the word "giant" as she and the students were reading together. Then she returned to it at the end of the sentence. She pointed out the picture clues and then directed the students' attention to the notion of Swimmy being an eye for a bigger fish made up of little fish. Finally, she had the students look at the initial letter "g" for the unknown word. The students quickly figured out "giant" from meaning clues. She had them practice with additional words in the story as they read along, to make sure they understood how to use the clues to figure out unknown words.

3. Independent practice.   To give her students independent practice, Mrs. Hoskins had the students read another story, in which she had placed gummed notes over some of the words in the text. She chose words in the students' oral vocabulary but not necessarily in their written vocabulary. On her notes, she gave the first letter as a cue for selecting the correct response.

Using *The Very Hungry Caterpillar,* by Eric Carle, the teacher replaced the covered words with "a" for apple on Monday, "p" for pears on Tuesday, "p" for plums on Wednesday, "s" for strawberries on Thursday, and "o" for oranges on Friday. The students wrote the missing words on notes as they read the passage. Mrs. Hoskins checked their work for differences in their answers.

4. Check for comprehension.   Later at reading conferences Mrs. Hoskins had students individually read and describe the semantic cueing strategy. In this direct lesson, the teacher used several word recognition skills, including semantics, phonics, and picture clues, to help students learn to uncover the unknown.

Teachers can help children use context clues even before they are readers. When reading books aloud to children, the teacher can occasionally leave off the last word of a sentence and invite the children to supply the word. For instance, if the book is about a child who is getting dressed to go out and play in the snow, the sentence might read: "August buttoned up her coat and then put on her _____." The children more than likely will end this sentence with "hat" or "gloves" or "mittens." This sort of practice helps students also when they are reading on their own. Using predictable books such as *Brown Bear, Brown Bear,* by Bill Martin, Jr., and other picture books help children predict and learn to recognize words. Because of the repetitive nature of this type of stories, children know what the words will be, so they match those words in their mind to the words on the page. The children are learning to use meaning-making words and pictures to help them figure out unknown words—semantic cueing.

Proficient readers use context clues without a second thought. When readers use the meaning of the surrounding text after skipping an unknown word or substituting another term during reading, and then return to figure out the word, they are using semantic and syntactic cues. Teachers can support the use of context clues by providing explicit and implicit practice for word recognition by the connection to meaning within the text or passage.

WHAT STRATEGIES CAN TEACHERS USE TO REINFORCE CONTEXT CLUES?

EXPANDING BACKGROUND

ALL

Building background provides students with the information they need to understand what they are reading. In her research, Stevens (1982) found that building background on a given topic enhances comprehension. Reading to children, taking field trips, encouraging parents to actively include their children in everyday experiences such as trips to the bank, grocery store, or shopping mall—all help develop children's understanding of the real world. An example of how a teacher can use background knowledge to help a child with context clues is to talk about a recent field trip to the zoo before reading a story about the zoo:

1. Ask the children to name the kinds of animals they saw at the zoo.
2. Write on chart paper the animal each child suggests, such as "zebra." Artistic teachers could draw a picture of a zebra on the chart paper. Or teachers could cut out and affix a picture of a zebra to the chart paper. (Having the student describe the zebra gives reminder clues to classmates on which animal is being discussed.)
3. Later, use the chart as a reference for the children and reread the zoo book together.

When the child encounters a new word, such as "hippopotamus," the child will be more apt to use semantic cues to figure out the word.

BASIC CLOZE

ALL

In a cloze activity, students are instructed to use context clues to fill in the blanks according to what makes sense based on their background knowledge and within the context of the passage. According to Choate, Enright, Miller, Poteet, and Rakes (1995), "The student must be able to pronounce or understand the meanings of the elements in order to select or produce the best elements to complete the sentences" (p. 131). To prepare a cloze for this purpose:

1. Choose a short text that is relatively easy for the students to read.
2. Type the text with every fifth word deleted and a blank line inserted in its place.
3. Have students read the text, filling in the blank with the words they think make sense.

When using this activity to practice using context clues with the whole class or in small groups, the teacher can read the text aloud, stopping at the blank lines to allow the children to say the words they inserted. The teacher can listen for the various answers students provide to see if the words make sense. If the teacher hears a word that does not fit the context, he or she can stop and discuss why that word does not work in that context. Students enjoy this type of oral reading because they are helping to read the story by supplying every fifth word.

Teachers can vary this strategy. Instead of asking the whole group to supply the words, they instead ask two or three students to supply the words as they read. Students can be asked to compare the stories of the different students: Do they vary? If so, is it because different words were supplied in the blanks?

With this type of cloze activity, prepared solely to practice context clues, the answers students provide do not have to exactly match the original text. If the word a student provides makes sense in context of the rest of the text, it is "right." Students who can supply several different "correct" words in the blanks are exhibiting strong use of context clues. This can be a sign of a proficient reader.

ORAL CLOZE

PRIMARY
INTERMEDIATE

In a slight variation of the cloze, which children often view as a game, teachers simply read aloud, stopping at certain words to let the children guess what word may come next. Teachers then talk about why the words the children chose make sense and help them understand why.

For example, when Mr. Salant was reading *Miss Nelson Has a Field Day,* by James Marshall, he read the sentence, "After rummaging around in her closet, she found what she was looking for—an ugly black _____." Every word the students guessed was a noun. They further used their knowledge of syntax to know what type of noun they were looking for. They knew that Miss Nelson found a "thing," not a person or a place.

PARTS-OF-SPEECH CLOZE

INTERMEDIATE
MIDDLE
SECONDARY
ESL

Teachers can design cloze exercises specifically to help older students practice syntactic cues for a variety of purposes. Teachers delete the specific parts of speech, for instance, to give students practice in using syntactic cues to reinforce learning more about the language. For example, in the sentence below, two nouns, an adjective, and a verb have been deleted.

In my family we like to walk in the park on beautiful fall days.

In my _____ we like to _____ in the _____ on _____ fall days.
      noun   verb   noun   adjective

Another variation is to create a cloze in which only specific parts of speech are omitted. For example, if a teacher is working on teaching verbs, she might create a cloze in which all or most of the verbs are deleted.

MATCHING CLOZE EXERCISE

ALL

The **matching cloze exercise** is identical to the cloze activity mentioned earlier except that, with the matching cloze, students receive a list of the deleted words, at the top or bottom of the page. Students can check off the words in the list as they use them to fill in the blanks. As with the regular cloze exercise, this activity helps students practice using their semantic and syntactic cueing skills.

MAZE EXERCISE

INTERMEDIATE
MIDDLE
SECONDARY
ESL

The maze exercise is similar to the cloze procedure except that, with the maze, students are given a list of three words to choose from, only one of which makes sense. This helps students use context clues to decide which word makes sense. Because making sense or deriving meaning is the heart of context clues, this exercise provides excellent practice for students who struggle with using context clues.

VARIATION. To use mazes to practice syntactic cues, the choice words can be similar except that they are different parts of speech. Only one word will make sense and be the part of speech that fits, as in the example below.

ALL

        beauty
It was a <u>beautiful</u> day in the Ozarks.
        because

INCREASING CONVERSATIONS

ALL

Talking with children is beneficial in building vocabulary and in developing language. Strickland and Morrow (1989) stated, "Oral language is a vehicle for the development of writing and reading" (p. 19). Lapp, Flood, Ranck-Buhr, VanDyke, and Spacek (1997) wrote, "Children's reading and writing processes develop through interactions with adults and peers" (p. 9). Teachers can encourage meaningful talk in classrooms by talking about things such as books, activities in the school and in the community, sporting events, or simply everyday activities in the classroom. These conversations will help students build background knowledge and thereby strengthen their use of semantic cues when reading.

MAD-LIBS

INTERMEDIATE
MIDDLE
SECONDARY
ESL

Mad-libs is a fun game in which short stories are written with blanks placed strategically throughout. Under each blank is the name of a part of speech, such as *noun* or *adjective*. Without reading the story, students are asked to give the teacher words that match the part of speech. The teacher writes the words on the lines and then reads the stories aloud to the class. The stories are often funny because, even if the part of speech is correct, the meaning may be silly. For this reason, the mad-libs activity provides good practice for syntactic cues rather than semantic cues. Teachers can create their own mad-lib short stories or purchase mad-libs. Here is an example:

The _____ went to the _____ for a _____ cup of soup for
   noun   noun   adjective

_____. When Jared arrived at _____, he _____ up and down.
 noun   noun   verb

WORD MIX-UP

ALL

An effective way to help students practice syntactic skills is to write a sentence on a piece of paper and then cut out each individual word. Students are to put the sentence in the correct order or an order that makes sense. For example, if Cathy were given the words "wants, to, to, fair, Joe, go, the," and she made the sentence, "Joe wants to go to the fair," her teacher would know that Cathy has a good understanding of syntax.

WHAT STRATEGIES CAN STUDENTS USE TO REINFORCE CONTEXT CLUES?

CROSS-CHECKING

ALL

Students can use the cross-checking strategy to help them understand what they have read. When students encounter an unknown word, they can go back and reread the sentence to see if it makes sense. If it does, they read on; if it does not, they look more closely to see what does not make sense. Teachers can demonstrate how students can use this strategy by putting sentences on the board and then covering one word in the sentence. The students read the sentence and then try to supply the covered-up word. This teaches the students how to use the other words in the sentence to figure out unknown words. Teacher modeling of this strategy helps students know how to use it when they are reading on their own.

TEMPORARILY SKIPPING THE UNKNOWN WORD

ALL

Skipping the unknown word and reading to the end of the sentence is an important fix-up strategy in reading comprehension, and particularly important in semantic cueing. When teachers model this strategy, students will learn to use it when they are reading on their own, and they learn to read to find out the meaning based on the whole text meaning.

APPLYING CLAY'S 5-FINGER SUGGESTION

ALL

In Clay's 5-finger suggestion (see page 41), her fourth suggestion for figuring out an unknown word is to read on to see if that will give the reader further clues. This is an example of using context clues. When Stephanie read, "The boy was exhausted because he didn't get enough sleep," she could not figure out the word "exhausted" until she had read the rest of the sentence. Then she knew what it meant.

READING ALOUD

ALL

When students come to an unknown word, it may help to read the entire sentence aloud to see if it sounds right. Because of their knowledge of language and sentence structure, they often can tell whether a word sounds right. A creative way in which some teachers help students hear themselves read is to bring in elbow pieces of plastic plumbing pipe (PVC pipe). The students hold one end to their ear and one end to their mouth. As they read into the pipe, they are able to hear themselves easily while other students in the class cannot.

REREADING

ALL

When students read a sentence that does not make sense, they can reread the sentence to see if the words sound right. If they read it and it sounds right but it still does not make sense (such as substituting "horse" for "house"), the students may use other clues such as context clues.

ASSESSMENT: HOW ARE CONTEXT CLUES ASSESSED?

Informal Reading Inventory

As discussed in Unit 1, many commercially prepared IRIs are available. When meaning (comprehension) breaks down while a student is reading a graded passage, the teacher may ascertain whether the student has the skills to figure out unknown words based on context clues. If the skills are not evident, the teacher may want to use the strategies given earlier for reinforcing context clues. Likewise, a teacher may use the results of an IRI to find out which strategies (also given earlier) students are using on their own to keep the meaning/comprehension ongoing.

Running Record

One component of a running record helps a teacher evaluate how the "child gathers up cues from the . . . meaning of the message" (Clay, 1993, p. 22). When a child self-corrects a word while reading, or goes back to reread a phrase, the teacher can tell if the student is using context clues to figure out the unknown word.

Cloze Procedure

The cloze procedure works well in assessing students' ability to use context clues because students have to look at the rest of the words in the sentence to figure out an unknown word. For example, when Jason read the sentence, "The boy's _____ hurt after drinking the _____ liquid," he could use context clues to fill in the first blank with "stomach" or "throat" and the second blank with "hot" or "spoiled." If Jason used words that did not make any sense at all, the teacher would know that he has trouble with context clues.

As an assessment of students' ability to use syntactic cues, teachers can choose the type of cloze exercise in which every nth word is deleted. For this type of assessment, students would not have to supply the exact word from the original text as long as they provided the correct part of speech.

Checklist

Through a checklist, a teacher may identify semantic or syntactic cues in which a student is excelling and is deficient. For example, an analysis of the results might indicate that a student (or small group of students) needs instruction in using context clues.

Anecdotal Record

By observing and recording reading behaviors, a teacher may notice the use of semantic and syntactic cues in word recognition skills. Instruction then leads to teaching strategies such as use of context clues, skipping the unknown word and reading to the end of the sentence to encourage independence in word recognition.

Asking Questions about Content

Another method that teachers can use to assess students' ability to use semantic cues "involves asking students questions about the words and word elements in a passage after they read orally or silently" (Choate et al., p. 131). Teachers can ask questions such as, "What did the main character, Carlos, mean when he said he was angry?" or "How could you tell that Carlos had ridden his bike to his grandmother's house?" Having the student describe what clues the text provided indicates how well the reader is using semantics. If readers can pick out several examples that led to their discovering the meaning of the unknown word, they are applying semantic cueing.

Another method is to ask questions that refer students back to a previous paragraph to figure out the meaning. By asking questions, a teacher can find out if a student is able to use semantic cues to determine unknown words.

Listening to Students Read

When teachers listen to students read, the teachers can tell whether students understand syntax by listening to the type of word miscues the students make. If they misread a noun but use another noun in its place, the teacher will know that students are using syntactic cues. If, for example, in the sentence, "A boy lost his kite," the student says "keep" instead of "kite," it is a good indication that the student might benefit from strengthening the use of syntactic cues.

Writing

As with other word recognition skills, context clues can be assessed by looking at students' writing. If a student wrote the sentence, "The ball red was bouncing," the teacher would know that this child needs help in understanding grammar and word order in a sentence.

2.4 Sight Words and Vocabulary: Do I Know This Word?

WHAT ARE SIGHT WORDS AND VOCABULARY?

Sight words have been defined as words that are immediately recognized as a whole and do not require word analysis for identification, or words taught as a whole (Harris & Hodges, 1995, p. 233). Words taught as a whole usually are learned by sight because they are phonetically irregular, such as "said" and "was." Others are of such high frequency (see Appendix E for a list) that they should simply be memorized, as "and" and "but." McCourt-Lewis (1980) defines sight vocabulary as "a body of words each of whose pronunciation is instantaneously available to the reader when s/he encounters the printed symbol" (p. 6).

Sight vocabulary, then, is a body of words that a reader knows instantly, the size of which is always increasing. When a reader has accumulated a large body of sight words, reading text becomes easier and, therefore, comprehension improves. If the reader must take time to decode individual letters and sounds, the sense of the text is often lost until the unknown word(s) can become a sight word and that is quickly identified. Thus, "automatic decoding frees the reader to process meaning" (McCourt-Lewis, 1980, p. 5). For students to become automatic readers, they need to memorize some words that do not decode easily.

HOW ARE SIGHT WORDS AND VOCABULARY TAUGHT?

Instruction in sight word vocabulary is carried out daily in almost all classrooms. The number of sight words can be increased through incidental learning—learning that is not intentionally taught—or by direct instruction—explicit teaching of a word. Children often acquire vocabulary during self-selected reading or recreational reading as they explore new texts and as they talk with others. Educators can take advantage of incidental learning by using teachable moments during classroom instruction.

Incidental learning of sight words can come from environmental print. For example, the "M" in the golden arches reminds children of the restaurant "McDonald's." Other examples are the "stop" on a sign that has eight sides and is red and white, and the lighted "exit" above a door in a movie theater. Reading in this way depends heavily upon visual cues. But, the "visual cues selected are only arbitrarily related to the words and must be rote memorized" (Scott and Ehri, 1990, p. 151). Therefore, incidental learning of sight words in this way uses memory of shapes, colors, and patterns rather than more general decoding rules. At some point, children must transfer "stop" surrounded by the colors of red and white to "stop" written on any background color. This happens with enough practice. Teachers can take advantage of incidental learning by labeling objects around their rooms and school. Creating environmental print picture books and adding examples to the word wall also support incidental learning. The key is to provide or promote natural examples that may not be taught formally in a lesson.

The importance of direct instruction should be remembered in vocabulary development as a part of word recognition. Direct instruction of sight words consists of the systematic, explicit, and deliberate teaching of words. Students may learn new words by looking them up or by having the definition given to them. Learning new words is more effective when first practicing them and applying them to new contexts. Careful selection of instructional methods when teaching new vocabulary is important. The traditional approach of giving children a list of words to look up, define, and use in a sentence does not provide real-world application of the terms; consequently, it does not enhance long-term memory. Direct instruction should be motivating, interesting, meaningful, and fun for students.

Direct instruction could be in the form of categorizing or grouping words for some reason (for example, winter words, vacation words, math terms). Usually, grouping words according to categories makes learning the individual words easier. Frequent review and use of sight words through reading or writing activities reinforces the learning of selected vocabulary.

Critical for emergent readers is teachers' direct instruction for meaning (vocabulary) and pronouncing (decoding) strategies. Attention should be directed to words the children will use repeatedly as they become fluent readers. For more experienced readers, the words selected should increase their abilities to communicate as adults.

Building students' sight words and vocabulary is an ongoing, daily emphasis. Therefore, incidental and direct instruction of sight words are both important in developing readers' ability to add new words to their growing vocabulary. High-frequency words (see Appendix E for a list) are chosen because they appear often in reading material for a selected grade level. Of the many high-frequency word lists available, several are based on Fry's List of "Instant Words" (Fry, 1977, p. 73). In upper-level classrooms the words encountered most frequently tend to be words specific to subject areas.

WHAT STRATEGIES CAN TEACHERS USE TO REINFORCE SIGHT WORDS AND VOCABULARY?

One of the first things teachers have to decide is which words are important enough to be taught for the students' comprehension of the reading selection. Choosing words can be determined by deciding which words are unknown to most readers, which words are most interesting, or which words can be transferred from one reading selection to another. Experience at any grade level allows teachers to know which words readers typically do not know and which words are most useful for that grade level.

Teachers can use the strategies below to teach and reinforce sight words and vocabulary. Often a strategy can be used to initially teach the sight word, and then by readers for reinforcement of the word.

VOCABULARY SELF-COLLECTION STRATEGY

One way to vary the traditional method of having the teacher list the vocabulary words while the students look them up is to have students pick out the vocabulary words as a vocabulary self-collection strategy (Haggard, 1986).

1. Divide the class into groups and have each group pick one vocabulary word from the text.

2. Have each group share its word (perhaps by writing it on the overhead projector transparency or chalkboard) and read the sentence containing the text, tell the group's definition of the word, and finally justify why the group chose the word.

According to Vacca and Vacca (1999), "As a result of the repeated use of the strategy, students learn how to make decisions related to the importance of concepts and how to use context to determine what words mean" (p. 63).

CONCEPT CIRCLES

Concept circles are a visual way for students to recognize vocabulary terms.

1. Draw a circle and divide it into four quadrants.
2. Write a related vocabulary word or term in each quadrant. (See Figure 2.3.)
3. Ask students to tell the general category for the words.

As a variation, instead of all of the words in the circle fitting into one category, include one term that does not relate. Students are to cross out the word that does not fit with the other three.

READ ALOUD DAILY

Reading aloud is one of the most effective strategies to increase the vocabulary of students over time. According to Anderson, Hiebert, Scott, and Wilkinson (1985), "The single most important activity for building the knowledge required for eventual success in reading is reading aloud to children" (p. 23). Daily teacher read-alouds put verbal words into students' listening and speaking vocabularies. Then students can more easily go a step further and identify the written word in their own reading, thereby adding the word to their sight vocabulary.

Reading to students is beneficial at all grade levels. Mr. Blakemore, a high school history teacher, reads books such as the *Biography of Benjamin Franklin* to his students several times a week. By reading books based on history, he is helping build students' vocabularies and getting them used to words they might encounter frequently when reading social studies texts.

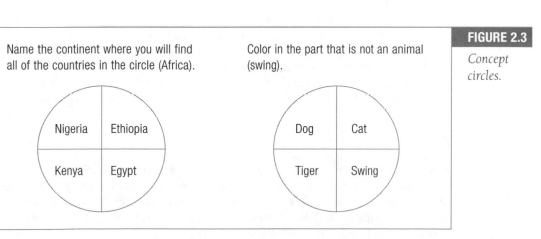

FIGURE 2.3

Concept circles.

WORD WALLS

PRIMARY
INTERMEDIATE

Sight words often are added to word walls as reminders to students. Word walls, in general, are made up of selected words attached to a wall in the classroom. These words typically are chosen because they contain spelling patterns or onsets and rimes that readers frequently encounter at a particular grade level. For example, "make" might be a word known to second graders, so it would be put on the word wall. Students then could read and spell other words such as "take," "cake," and "lake." Mrs. Carnagey helps students identify rimes on the word wall by placing a star beside a word that can be used to make other words. For example, a star beside "an" would indicate that consonants can be added at the beginning to make words such as can, tan, ran, fan, and man.

MIDDLE
SECONDARY
ESL

VARIATION. Word walls in the upper grades can include terminology from specific subject areas. For example, in Mr. Burnhart's chemistry class, every time students encounter a new term, he has them add it to a bulletin board especially for that purpose.

FOCUS ON INTERESTING WORDS

ALL

Another way of enlarging students' sight vocabulary is to teach explicitly words that readers find interesting. For example, the word "parradiddles" in *Taste of Blackberries* (by Dorothy B. Smith) might appeal to fourth graders because it is an interesting word that sounds silly. Students can predict how to pronounce it and what it means based on context clues including semantic cues and syntactic cues. In class discussions readers can share their own interesting words from a selection.

WORD GAMES

PRIMARY

Word games are fun for students and at the same time reinforce sight words and vocabulary. Games might include Word Bingo or Word Fishing. Word Bingo is played just like the regular Bingo except that instead of numbers on the card, the cards contain sight words. The teacher calls out a sight word and the students put a game piece on that word on their card.

With Word Fishing, sight words are written on individual cards that have a magnet attached to them. The students use a "fishing pole" with a magnet attached on a string to fish for a card. When they pull up a card, they read the sight word. Playing this game fosters students' knowledge of words while they learn to play fairly, take turns, and win or lose a game with dignity. Games can be purchased, or teachers can make their own games and game boards.

WORD SORTS

PRIMARY

In word sorts, words are sorted or grouped into various categories. These can be categorized as either open sorts or closed sorts. When students are introduced to word sorts, teachers may want to designate the desired heading to focus on skills being taught and also to model how the list can be sorted into several categories. In a closed sort, students are asked to sort groups of words according to a predetermined set of categories. For example, students are asked to sort a list of farm-related terms by objects found in a barn, in the field, and in a farmhouse. In an open sort, students are asked to group words and explain the categories they represent. For example, if a list of animals is given, students might choose to sort farm animals, zoo animals, four- or two-legged animals, feathered or furry animals. The same list of animals could be sorted by the number of syllables in each word or by the beginning letters of the word.

VARIATION. In a middle school or secondary English class, words such as "sonnets, haiku, essays, limericks, poetry, novels, and biographies" might be contained in the list of words to be sorted. In a closed sort, the heading might be "prose or poetry." Using an open sort, students may select their own headings for these words (and defend their reasoning), such as short poems, long poems, fiction, and nonfiction.

INTERMEDIATE
MIDDLE
SECONDARY
ESL

WORD HUNTS

The word hunt is an excellent strategy for reinforcing sight vocabulary. The teacher might hunt for familiar words in a passage that rhyme with *ight* in "sight," or find "fight" and "light" in the selection. After sharing a reading selection, the teacher chooses a spelling pattern (or phonic generalization) found in several words in the selection. Students then hunt for other words from familiar books, word walls, or wall charts that fit that generalization. These words can be written on chart paper, added to often, and reviewed frequently.

PRIMARY
INTERMEDIATE

VARIATION. Similarly, high school history students might look for words such as *communism, socialism,* and *capitalism* in their government textbooks or political magazines.

MIDDLE
SECONDARY
ESL

WORD OF THE DAY

Many teachers and students like the idea of presenting a new word every day.

INTERMEDIATE
MIDDLE
SECONDARY
ESL

1. Write a "new" word on the chalkboard or on a piece of paper and tape it to the door.
2. Begin the day by asking students to guess what the word means, discuss why they think so, or explain where they have heard the word before.
3. Read the word in a sentence to give the students clues that will help them figure out the meaning.
4. After the word is defined, encourage students to use it in sentences of their own.

Teachers can use any word or look for specific words that students will encounter in their studies that week. For example, if the class is beginning a study of the Civil War, the word of the week might be "antebellum." Because the teacher introduces this word early in the study of the Civil War, each time students encounter the word, they attain a better understanding of what it means. Soon they will know the word automatically; it will become a word they know by sight. Many teachers find that using challenging words is particularly effective in vocabulary building.

KINESTHETIC ACTIVITIES

PRIMARY

For children who learn best by movement, teachers can use activities such as clapping or snapping fingers for each letter in the word as the word is said or chanted aloud. Or gross motor movements can represent the height of letters in words. For example, "dog" would be represented by stretching the arms and hands high overhead to represent the above-the-line letter "d." Touching the shoulders with the hands could represent the on-the-line letter "o." Arms stretched straight down at the sides could represent the below-the-line letter "g." These activities also can help teachers assess children's knowledge of the words.

WHAT STRATEGIES CAN STUDENTS USE TO REINFORCE SIGHT WORDS AND VOCABULARY?

READ SILENTLY OR ALOUD

ALL

Reading, either silently or aloud, makes better readers. *Becoming a Nation of Readers,* by Anderson, Hiebert, Scott, and Wilkinson (1985) states, "Reading . . . is not something that is mastered once and for all at a certain age. Rather, it is a skill that continues to improve through practice" (p. 16). Readers read easy, familiar books for review and reinforcement of sight words and also should be encouraged to stretch themselves to read more challenging material.

PARALLEL BOOKS

PRIMARY
INTERMEDIATE
MIDDLE
ESL

After reading a book, students write and illustrate a **parallel book** that uses some or much of the original text or structure of the story. For example, *If You Give a Moose a Muffin,* by Laura Joffe Numeroff, can be changed to, *If You Give a Dog a Doughnut.* One word that students can practice is "finished," as in "When he's finished with it, he'll want . . . ." Students should be given the opportunity to present their creative pieces to classmates. By sharing their books, students will be seeing the same words again and again—an excellent way to practice sight vocabulary.

WORD DICTIONARIES, BANKS, BOXES

ALL

Individual readers record words they need or want to know to be better spellers. These collections can be alphabetized in spiral notebooks (one page for each letter of the alphabet) or an index card box, or held together by a notebook ring. Students may add words as needed and use them in spelling and writing activities. After repeated use, the words become part of their sight words.

WORD COLLECTIONS

MIDDLE
SECONDARY
ESL

Just as younger students create word banks or word boxes, older students can start word collections. Many students enjoy collecting objects such as stamps, coins, or sports cards. In the same way, they can collect new words. Eleventh grader Joe got interested in new words after taking his high school word study class. As he started noticing new and interesting words, he began to write them in the back of one of his class notebooks. He enjoys seeing how many unusual words he has discovered.

ASSESSMENT: HOW DO WE ASSESS SIGHT WORDS AND VOCABULARY?

Informal Reading Inventory

IRIs have reading passages that are useful for assessing sight vocabulary within context. Most IRIs include questions to ask students after they have finished a retelling, with one question strictly about vocabulary.

Children's Literature

Children's literature provides appropriate text material on a wide variety of topics, both fiction and nonfiction. Asking students to read from their favorite books is an excellent way to assess sight words. Teachers must be sure that students are matching written words to spoken words, not merely retelling the story or using the illustrations as clues. Teachers can check to see if students really know the words by pointing to the words (out of order) to see if students can pronounce the words. In the book *It Looked Like Spilt Milk,* by Charles Shaw, Melissa looked at the picture while remembering the text her teacher read. Melissa "read" the illustrations, matching printed text with verbal words. As she encountered the words, "It looked like spilt milk" on every other page, she soon had learned the words by sight. Her teacher then pointed to "spilt," "wasn't," and "sometimes" to verify that Melissa had learned the words.

Word Wall Activities

Using word wall activities daily reinforces the words and also aids teachers in assessing students' acquisition of selected words. One activity is to provide students with clues to a preselected word. For example, Mrs. Stapleton says, "I'm thinking of a word on the word wall that begins like 'mother,' has four letters, and rhymes with 'soon.'" The students respond by writing the word "moon" on their paper or board or by raising their hand.

Writing

Teachers can assess whether or not students are learning new sight words and vocabulary by watching to see if they incorporate the new words in their writing. If students can use the words, then the words have become part of their vocabularies. Before beginning a writing assignment, teachers can tell students to look through their personal word banks and word collections and encourage them to use some of their new words in their writing. Teachers can then assess whether or not the students used the words correctly.

Supporting SKILLS

For students to be successful in life, they have to become independent readers. For this reason, parents and the American public have expressed growing interest in having children acquire strong word recognition skills. During school hours teachers can support and scaffold students' learning. Harris and Hodges (1995) defined *scaffolding* as "the gradual withdrawal of adult (e.g., teacher) support, as through instruction, modeling, question, feedback, etc., for a child's performance across successive engagements, thus transferring more and more autonomy to the child" (p. 226).

One way teachers provide scaffolding is by teaching students how to use supporting skills such as previewing, visual clues, dictionary skills, reference skills, and use of technology. Then students know what sources to use later in life when a teacher is not available. Students learn how to find their own information. This is an important piece in helping students become independent readers.

The ability and desire to read for pleasure and recreation and to read in real-world activities (check writing, notes to family and friends) are what ultimately influence the lifelong reading habit. Although teachers cannot be in con-

stant contact with students, they can teach, model, practice, and review several supporting skills in the classroom. These skills, along with the word recognition skills described frequently, allow students to become truly independent in all areas of reading.

3.1 Previewing

Previewing text material before actually reading it is one of the most powerful prereading skills by which students can enhance their comprehension. In fact, Spargo (1974) claims that the single most important technique you can acquire in any reading course is the habit of previewing (p. 14). Previewing, or surveying the text, gives students an idea of the content of the written material, a mindset about the reading selection. This skill can be taught and modeled in the classroom for all types of reading, including recreational reading and content-area text reading.

Students can be taught to scan or skim the reading selection by quickly looking over the text. In **scanning** a text, readers look over the text quickly, hunting for specific information. For example, when looking for a certain phone number in the phone book, a reader does not read every name but instead looks for one specific name. When **skimming**, the reader glances over the text to get a quick overview. An example of this is the way a person reads the newspaper. The reader typically reads the headings and captions quickly, looking for articles of most interest to read.

The same strategy can be applied to reading a textbook assignment. If the text is a social studies chapter, for example, students can be encouraged to read the introductory paragraphs and the concluding paragraphs to connect background knowledge to new, unknown material. The students can look at pictures and illustrations and read the captions, read words that are italicized or bolded, and read the headings. Teachers can point out new vocabulary words. After getting a general idea of what the chapter is about, students can read the entire selection to fill in the blanks of their knowledge.

If the text is narrative, such as a novel or story, students can do a picture-walk through the text or read any text printed on the book covers. With all types of texts, students can read the preface, introduction, and table of contents. This type of prereading or previewing gives students clues as to what the book is about and helps with comprehension.

STRATEGIES TO TEACH PREVIEWING

ACTIVATING PRIOR KNOWLEDGE

PRIMARY
INTERMEDIATE
ESL

Teachers can help students activate their prior knowledge on the subject they are preparing to read.

1. Begin by asking questions about the book cover, any pictures in the text, illustrations, diagrams, or charts.
2. Connect to students' prior knowledge by asking what they already know about the subject.
3. Follow up by asking predicting questions about what the students might learn or find in the text.

4. Read the text to confirm the predictions and connect to prior experiences.

For example, at the elementary level, before reading *Everybody Cooks Rice,* by Norah Dooley, the teacher can ask the students how many of their families eat rice. The students then discuss how their families cook rice. Do they have fried rice? White rice? Do they buy it in a box? After students have had an opportunity to discuss rice, the teacher can suggest that students scan the book, looking at the pictures to see if they can spot some examples of ways to cook rice other than those mentioned already. Participating in prereading activities like this one helps activate students' prior knowledge on the subject, thereby making the reading more meaningful.

VARIATION. Students in upper grades can benefit from previewing material to be read in textbooks. Before assigning a chapter on the effects of smoking cigarettes for a health class, the teacher can "walk" the students through the chapter, talking about things such as a picture of a damaged lung or a chart showing the percentages of people who smoke who get lung cancer. Teachers also can introduce students to new vocabulary they might encounter in the text. Discussions such as these help students comprehend better when they read the text.

INTERMEDIATE
MIDDLE
SECONDARY
ESL

SQ3R

Previewing is a major component in the method SQ3R (Robinson, 1961).

INTERMEDIATE
MIDDLE
SECONDARY
ESL

1. Before students read the text, have them *survey (S)* the text meaning by quickly glancing over the table of contents, introduction, headings, captions, and so forth to get an overview of what the text is about.
2. Have the students turn each heading into a *question (Q)*. Example: For the heading "Extinct Animals of the World," students might ask, "What animals of the world are extinct?"
3. Have the students *read (R)* the section. In the example above, the students read only the section on extinct animals.
4. Have the students *recite (R)* the answers to their questions through a process such as reciting aloud, notetaking, or underlining. In the example above, students answer their question about what animals are extinct.
5. Continue this process of question, read, recite throughout the rest of the chapter or assignment.
6. Have the students *review (R)* the entire material by looking over their notes or questions, to move the material to long-term memory.

ANTICIPATION GUIDES

Anticipation guides provide an excellent means for helping students to preview a text. An anticipation guide is a set of sentences that students respond to before reading a text.

INTERMEDIATE
MIDDLE
SECONDARY
ESL

1. Create a set of statements based upon the major points or ideas in a text.
2. Place statements in a format that requires students to anticipate or predict a response.

3. Have students circle T (true) or F (false) based on their anticipation.
4. Prior to reading, discuss students' predictions.
5. Have students read the selection and confirm their anticipation guide responses.
6. Contrast the predictions with the correct answers.

EXAMPLE OF ANTICIPATION GUIDE

1. (T) F   Camels are mammals.   3. T (F) All mammals breathe with lungs.
2. T (F) Mammals lay eggs.   4. (T) F Mammals have live births.

In this example, the student's choices are circled. The correct answers are T, F, T, T. During the reading and then in the discussion, the student learned that all mammals breathe with lungs.

K-W-L

ALL

The K-W-L strategy, developed by Ogle (1986), is a simple procedure that helps students preview, as well as remind them of, what they already know about the subject.

1. Draw the chart shown below on the chalkboard, chart paper, or overhead projector transparency.
2. In the first column, *What do we know? (K),* record what is already known about the topic—prior knowledge.
3. In the *What do we want to know? (W)* column, generate and list questions the students and teacher come up with.
4. Read the text selection, keeping the questions in mind.
5. In the *What we learned (L)* column, add information students have gleaned from the text.

Jessica's third graders were working in a unit on folktales, and she used the K-W-L strategy to introduce "Story of the Three Little Javelinas," by Susan Lowell. Part of the class chart is given below.

K	W	L
(What do we know?)	(What do we want to know?)	(What we learned)
"Lon Po Po" is another folktale	What are javelinas?	
Many folktales are about animals, and they talk.	Do all folktales have animals in them?	
Folktales have morals, or a lesson is learned.	What is the lesson in this story?	

Ogle suggests that students focus on the questions and information generated and predict the categories to be included in the text.

3.2 Visual Clues

isual clues might include pictures and illustrations, captions, graphs, tables, charts, or other graphics. Teachers should emphasize to students that the reading selections contain visuals for a purpose, not just to take up space on the page. Visual clues are used to organize or otherwise extend information contained in the written text material. Visual learners may be able to retain information better through this picture/graphic format.

Often, before children learn that symbols on a page represent words, they learn that pictures and illustrations on a page represent stories. Next they learn that illustrations can help them figure out what those symbols or words stand for. Vocabulary terms often can be illustrated to help students better understand how the word can be used.

Picture books, of course, get their name from the extensive use of illustrations to support the written text. Young children and nonreaders often "read" the story by looking at the pictures. The illustrations usually are placed on the same page as the written text. Teachers of emergent readers can use picture clues to help these readers figure out new words.

For example, when John was reading a book and came to the word "toad," he looked at the picture of the toad and said "frog." Even though he did not get the exact word, he was using picture clues to figure it out. When he said "frog," the teacher replied, "Does frog start with a 't?'" John looked back at the word and started sounding out the word by saying "to -," then shouted "toad!" He was using picture clues and phonics to figure out "toad."

Beginning readers use picture clues while they are learning other word recognition skills such as phonics, context clues including semantics and syntax, and structural analysis. As children get older, they use illustrations in books for recreational reading, and their textbooks are smaller, more detailed, and usually less colorful because students who have learned other word recognition skills no longer need picture clues. In textbooks for upper grades, illustrations frequently do not appear on the same page as the written description. Older students who still rely on illustrations to help with text reading are frustrated because of the placement or size of the illustrations.

Visual clues usually have captions that further explain the purpose of the visual. For example, the caption for an illustration of a lady with a flag stretched out on her lap and onto the floor might read: "Betsy Ross sewing together the first American flag." The teacher should point out that captions help readers understand what the visual is and why it is located at that point in the text.

Graphs, tables, and charts are extremely useful for visual learners. Several pages of written text often are condensed into a single graph, table, or chart. Students need to be taught how to use these visuals, for example: how to "read" a pie graph to determine percentages of how household income is spent or a bar graph to determine how many people own dogs compared to how many own cats or birds; how to read a table to find out teachers' salaries in one state compared to other states; how to "read" a chart of weather fronts passing over the United States.

STRATEGIES TO TEACH VISUAL CLUES

TELLING THE STORY THROUGH PICTURES

ALL

To help early readers understand that pictures help to tell the story, the teacher can give children wordless picture books such as *Time Flies,* by Eric Rohmann, and have the students tell the story. The teacher writes the words as the children tell what happened in the book. The teacher cuts out the sentences the children say and tapes them to each page to fit what the students said for each picture. Then the teacher can go back and read the story to the children. This illustrates to the children how pictures and words fit together to tell a story.

Teachers of older students can ask them to explain in paragraph form what a graph or chart means. For example, students in a history class are given a graph showing the number of casualties from wars in which Americans have been involved. They use the graph to explain in words the number of casualties from each war. This exercise helps students articulate what graphs mean. Students also could create their own graphs.

CREATING ILLUSTRATIONS

PRIMARY

To help students understand the connections between words and illustrations, the teacher can have them create their own illustrations to match text. Younger students can draw pictures to go with a story they have read or written them-selves. For example, if the students wrote stories about animals they saw at the zoo on their recent class field trip, they could draw on the same page as their written work a picture of the animal.

INTERMEDIATE
MIDDLE
SECONDARY
ESL

VARIATION. Older students could be given a copy of a cartoon with the words in the conversation bubbles whited-out, and asked to write their own text to fit the illustrations. Students in a middle school or high school social studies class could be asked to read a political editorial and then write the text to fit a political cartoon.

3.3 Dictionary Skills

When students ask teachers to pronounce and define unknown words, the teachers often reply, "Look it up in the dictionary" because teachers want students to become independent readers. Use of a dictionary is one tool to aid students in that process. For a dictionary to become and remain useful, however, dictionary skills must be taught and supported throughout the curriculum. Like most skills, ongoing instruction and practice in using the dictionary are important. When young children are successful in using a pictionary (a dictionary with pictures) to correct spelling, define, or illustrate a word, it is easier to transfer that learning to the use of a more sophisticated dictionary. A wide range of types of dictionaries is available—from pictionaries to unabridged versions. Teachers must choose the types of dictionaries to use and match them to students' ability level and needs.

Dictionaries can be used to support reading strategies taught in classrooms. Probably the least effective use is to merely tell readers where the dictionary is located in the classroom and then leave students to use it whenever and however they want rather than to teach them the "how to's" of dictionary use. The former does not teach purpose or incentive to encourage students to take the time to learn to use the dictionary efficiently.

Three of the most important elements to teach students about the dictionary are: (1) locating words, (2) determining word pronunciation, and (3) determining word meaning and usage (Harris & Sipay, 1990).

Locating words.   Instruction in use of the dictionary should begin with the way a dictionary is organized—alphabetically by first letter, then by second letter, and so on. If the unknown word begins with the first part of the alphabet, the students are to open the dictionary toward the front. If using the computer, they are to scroll to the first part of the alphabet. If the word begins with a letter toward the end of the alphabet, the reverse is true.

Use of guidewords at the top of the pages is a timesaving skill. If the dictionary is on a computer, the desired letter can be indicated by a keystroke or by scrolling down to the letter. Once students learn how to look up words in the dictionary, they should receive ample practice so it becomes easier for them. The dictionary races strategy on the following page provides examples of how students can practice their dictionary skills.

Determining word pronunciation.   Learning how to use the pronunciation key in the dictionary entry will help independent readers decode unfamiliar written words, often by linking them to their listening vocabulary. A sample pronunciation key is found in Appendix F. Pronunciation keys at the bottom of each dictionary page provide easy words illustrating vowel and consonant sounds. Teachers could give students a short list of unknown words and model a think-aloud for how to use the pronunciation key (see page 17 for more information about think-alouds).

This important student strategy should be taught directly, and teachers also may take advantage of teachable moments to reinforce phonics. For example, students in a math class are reading about the metric system and want to know if "kilometer" is pronounced "ki-lam'-a-ter" or "kil'-a-met-er." Rather than just telling the students, the teacher might say, "Let's look it up together and see how to pronounce it." The teacher then can write on the board the two sound spellings from the dictionary and explain or remind students what the different symbols mean. The teacher also can explain that the two sounds spellings mean that both pronunciations are correct. Cunningham (as cited in Robinson, McKenna, & Wedman, 1996), found that having struggling readers find polysyllabic words in the dictionary and pronounce them added greatly to their word recognition.

Determining word meaning and usage.   Students also need to be taught how to figure out which word meaning is the one they are looking for. For example, if students want to know what the word "excavated" means in the sentence, "The bones were excavated and examined more closely," from the book *Graveyards of the Dinosaurs,* by Shelley Tanaka, they can use context clues to see which definition makes the most sense. They can tell by context clues that "to uncover or expose by digging" makes more sense than "to make a hole or cavity" or "to form by hollowing out."

Every unknown word may not have to be checked in the dictionary. If students can learn approximations of meanings from the context of the reading selection, they might not have to find them in a dictionary. For example, if sixth grader Cody were reading *A Taste of Blackberries* by Doris B. Smith, he might not know the term "allergic reaction." By reading further in the passage, however, he should be able to understand the meaning of the term enough to comprehend the story. Then, if he needs or wants further information, Cody can use a dictionary to learn more about the words "allergic" and "reaction."

Dictionaries should be accessible. If they are on the bottom of a back shelf in an out-of-the-way place covered by a layer of dust, students are not going to be eager to use them. More than one dictionary is preferred, with at least one near the teacher's desk. If the copyright date of the dictionary is not recent, the teacher should request newer editions to keep abreast of new terms such as those used in technology. Students may prefer small, handheld, computer-type dictionaries or CD-ROM editions for use on the computer. Both of these types may be more appealing to students than the more traditional book.

Besides the commercial dictionaries, teachers should encourage students to use personal or individual dictionaries. These may be in the form of a spiral notebook with one page for each letter of the alphabet, index cards with the words alphabetized in a file box, or alphabetized word cards with punched holes, held together by notebook rings. Some teachers call these *word banks* or *word boxes* (see page 60 for more information). As the term indicates, personal dictionaries contain words that individual students want or need to know how to spell. For example, Angie may have the word *house* in her personal dictionary, but Jessie may already know that word and, therefore, not include it in her dictionary.

STRATEGIES TO TEACH DICTIONARY SKILLS

DICTIONARY RACES

ALL

A dictionary race is a fun way for students to practice using a dictionary.

1. Give students their own copy of the dictionary.
2. Place the closed dictionary between their hands with the spine on their desk.
3. Say a predetermined word, then "go."
4. Have students race to find the word, put their finger on it, and stand up.
5. Designate the first five (or whatever number the teacher decides) to stand up as the winners.
6. Confirm the correct answer (teachers and students).

A way to vary the game so students compete with other students of their same ability level is to have the students sit in groups of five or six or in rows. After the first word, the winners all move to the same table. After each word, the winner in each group moves up a table and one of the students who did not win moves down a table to make room for the winner. The purpose is to have students compete with others of about the same ability so they have a better chance to win.

PRIMARY
INTERMEDIATE

VARIATION. When introducing the game to younger students, teachers can begin by saying "front," "middle," or "end" to teach students the concept of where to start when looking for a word. Then teachers progress to giving students just a letter rather than a whole word. Then when a teacher says "B—Go," students know they are to open to the "B" section. Then they add a second letter, such as "e." This progression teaches students which letters to look at next until they are able to find the whole word.

CREATING DICTIONARIES

One meaningful way to help students understand how dictionaries work is to have them create their own dictionaries. Mrs. Renkoski had her fifth grade students make a class dictionary, in which the students wrote their own entries about themselves. For their own page each student had to list the following.

1. Last name, first name. Their name had to be broken into syllables just as words are in the dictionary.
2. For sound spelling, they had to write their name using the sound spelling key in the dictionary.
3. For definitions 1, 2, and 3, they were to describe what they look like.
4. For 4, 5, and 6, they described their personality traits.
5. For 7, 8, 9, and 10, they had to tell four things they wanted to do when they grow up.
6. Then they included a picture of themselves.

Finally, Mrs. Renkoski put each page together in alphabetical order to form a class dictionary. Students also can make dictionaries of new words they are learning. As students add words to their word banks, they can include the sound spelling and a short definition.

WORD QUESTIONS

As a practice exercise, each student is given a list of questions using words from a content-area text or vocabulary words such as: Can you eat a *rhapsody?* Would a *litany* make a good pet? Can you give an example of an animal that *exuviates?* Students have to look up the word to know how to answer the question.

3.4 Reference Skills

Fiction books and stories are almost always read from beginning to end. Fiction is sometimes called "once upon a time . . . happily ever after" material. Reference materials, on the other hand, usually are not read from beginning to end. Students use different types of reference materials to meet their various needs. Students' ability to use reference materials effectively and efficiently allows them to become more independent in reading. Teachers should teach students to use reference materials by modeling their use in the classroom and also by specific and direct instruction in their use. Reference materials include items such as encyclopedias, textbooks, almanacs, and other nonfiction writing.

One outcome of effective reading instruction is for students to become independent readers, and reference materials are tools to that end. Teaching students to use the Table of Contents, Index, and Glossary in textbooks and reference materials helps them find information quickly. Students realize they can find out information on their own without waiting for the teacher or another adult to tell them what they want to know.

For example, if Joe wants to know the names of the planets in order beginning closest to the sun, he could ask a teacher or he could look up the information in a science text or an encyclopedia. This independence becomes increasingly important during the hours students are not in school. Knowing how to locate factual information using books and computer search engines is personally satisfying.

Students use higher-order thinking skills and a process for using reference material when they focus on an unknown piece of desired information, decide where the solution or answer might be located, know how to search through the reference material chosen (either a hard copy or an online search), eliminate the information that does not fit the need, then pull it all together to find the solution or answer. Because this process has many steps, teachers may use any or all of the steps to teach students valuable research skills. Most of the steps mentioned previously can be the objective of a lesson, or a more effective way might be to teach the use of reference skills as other lessons are taught. This is another way to teach across the curriculum.

The value of reference materials across the curriculum becomes apparent in the following scenario: During a study of nocturnal animals in science, bats in particular, and after a field trip to a cave to observe bats, Danielle wanted to know how many different types of bats there are in the world. Because of limited space, the science textbook can provide only a small amount of information. But the student was persistent. The teacher directed Danielle to several different sources of reference material to find out how many species of bats there are. *The World Almanac for Kids: 1999,* page 87 states that there are 1,000 species of bats and that "there are more species of bats than of any other mammal" (E. Israel, Editor). Later, Danielle might compare that information with other reference materials to see if the information is the same.

The world of children's literature is constantly expanding. "Within the past few years, there has been a virtual explosion of books published for children—both fiction and nonfiction" (Camp, 2000, p. 400). Teachers should capitalize on this and choose nonfiction books to extend textbook information. Because of limited space to cover a large range of information, a textbook cannot cover a topic in depth. That may be fine for some topics. Other topics might require more breadth and depth of information.

Children's literature provides an ideal way to do this. The creative text structure and illustrations in "informational books now available for children can make content-area material come alive" (Camp, 2000, p. 400).

Teachers should become familiar enough with children's literature to be able to choose nonfiction books that will augment and supplement content textbooks. Books such as the *Magic School Bus* series, by Joanna Cole, or Seymour Simon's beautifully illustrated books can engender the enthusiasm and excitement of almost any child.

STRATEGIES TO TEACH REFERENCE SKILLS

DATA BANKS

INTERMEDIATE
MIDDLE
SECONDARY

Instead of sending students to the encyclopedia and telling them to write a report on a certain topic, Lori Elliott provides her students with a sheet called a data bank (see Figure 3.1). Across the top of the page, students write the

DATA BANK TOPIC		FIGURE 3.1
Where does it live?	What does it eat?	*Sample data bank sheet.*
What does it do?	What does it have?	
What does it look like?	Extra information	

name of their topic, such as "Mountain Lion." Then, on the sheet they answer the following questions: Where does it live? What does it eat? What does it do? What does it have? What does it look like? Space is provided for extra information. Once students have filled out their data sheets, they can write their reports based on what they learned. Strategies such as these help students learn how to look for pertinent information rather than just copying from the book.

K-W-W-L

K-W-W-L is a strategy developed by Bryan (1998) based on **K-W-L**, developed by Ogle (1986). *K* stands for what students already *know* about a certain topic. The first *W* stands for *want*—"What do I *want* to know?" The second *W* is the part where students can practice their use of reference skills: It stands for *where*—"*Where* can I find the answers to my questions?" Finally, the L stands for *learned*—"What did I *learn?*" K-W-W-L helps learners to develop appropriate questions for research and to organize what they know, and it helps learners focus on where to locate specific information.

INTERMEDIATE
MIDDLE
SECONDARY
ESL

GRAPHIC ORGANIZERS

Students can use graphic organizers to help them organize the types of information they get from various reference materials. The example of a webbing graphic organizer in Figure 3.2 shows how students can gather multiple resources before writing a report.

INTERMEDIATE
MIDDLE
SECONDARY
ESL

FIGURE 3.2

Sample webbing graphic organizer.

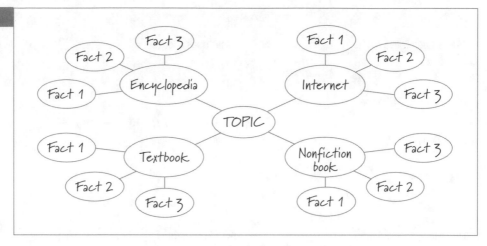

3.5 Technology

Teachers and students can use technology to enhance learning. Just as a hammer is the tool chosen for pounding nails more efficiently than trying to push nails into a board or by using the heel of a shoe to tap them in, selecting the appropriate technology to accomplish a learning goal is important. Technology is being infused throughout the school curriculum, as well as teacher preparation programs. With the growing interest in and use of technology in education, taking a look at the relationship between technology and word recognition skills makes sense.

Although computers are a vital part of the field of technology, they are not the only facet. From overhead projectors to tape recorders to satellite link-ups, technology is on the rise in schools. Some of the challenges teachers face in implementing technology in their classrooms include selecting the appropriate technology, finding the resources, and designing appropriate instructional procedures. Because "reading is an interactive process in which readers call upon both visual and nonvisual sources of information to make sense of the text" (Zakaluk & Sealey, 1988, p. 93), technologies may effectively support reading and comprehension through the development of word recognition skills. This section provides an overview of related technology, the technologies that support word recognition, and the practice and implementation of related skills. Before integrating technology into their classrooms, teachers should consider several issues.

TRAINING

Are educators prepared to use technology? Teacher preparation programs at most institutions include learning about and through a variety of media. Multimedia experiences often provide more authentic learning and teaching opportunities. Educators may be exposed to a variety of learning situations themselves through classes or workshops offered through ITV and by using the Internet to research information. Guided practice during coursework can help prepare teachers for future technology-rich classrooms, and inservice teachers may avail themselves of professional development opportunities or graduate classes to further their understanding and application of new technologies in their classrooms.

Whether teachers have formal training or "jump in with both feet" and learn through trial and error, understanding the technology and how to use it efficiently and appropriately is vital. For example, Lois wanted to show her class a video clip from her new communication arts curriculum of an author reading a story using the laserdisc machine. She had the equipment delivered to her room, but when it came time to find the clip, she could not find the right spot. Instead of scanning in the bar code, as she had witnessed a presenter do at a conference, her school's projector called for her to type in the clip code. Precious learning time was wasted because Lois was not well trained.

CONSISTENCY

Is the technology consistent with the educator's teaching philosophy, style, and goals? Choosing technology based on students' needs and teachers' expectations for their learning can support teaching. If a teacher adheres to a constructivist approach to teaching, students in the classroom will be adding to their own word banks constantly as they hear and use words from their environment. Making-words activities are supportive of word building, using affixes, identifying word parts and roots, and implementing decoding strategies.

Tenisha found an interactive CD-ROM in her reading curriculum supplemental resources that allowed children to practice building new words. She was excited because it offered three levels of practice. The technology offered Tenisha a way to provide remediation for some students, enrichment for others, and fun but effective practice for still others. She was able to reach more students and address their individual needs better than if she had provided only worksheets.

ACCESSIBILITY

Do educators have access to technology? Things usually go wrong when least expected, so access is important. Although computers in the classroom and schools have created more educational opportunities, accessibility can be a major concern. How can a teacher use one computer effectively with 30 children? How effective is the computer lab when 20 classes have to share it equally? What if a school cannot afford a computer teacher to staff the lab?

A three-to-one ratio is appropriate for student interaction and learning when learners share a computer (Piper, 1998). The cost of more computers often prohibits more than one per classroom, and scheduling effective use of the computer(s) becomes a challenge. Creating a computer lab for an entire school to use limits the accessibility, and sometimes instruction. Teachers cannot make use of teachable moments using the computer or plan for routine use if students have to walk to the opposite end of the school. If obstacles are overcome, however, using the computer can be exciting and helpful in developing word recognition skills for students.

Using the technology available in your classroom and school building wisely is the first challenge. Creating centers for children to use materials regularly, checking out equipment early for reviewing or prompting, ordering new resources well in advance of their planned use, and combining allocations for purchasing power are worth the minimal extra work in the planning stages.

Availability was an issue when Vern discovered a website on the computer that offered a matching game of sounds for young children. He prepared the lesson, signed up his class for the computer lab, and prepared his students. Unfortunately, Vern did not account for the 11:00 A.M. rush on the Internet by the district, and the system lines were too busy to connect all of the computers. The computer teacher, Sheila, however, had a similar activity already installed on the computers in the lab, which she was able to open quickly for the first graders.

APPROPRIATENESS

Is the selected technology age-, grade-, and content-appropriate? The computer should be thought of as a teaching tool or addition to learning, not the entire instructional program. From a review of research studies, Piper (1998) indicated that using the computer to assist students in phonological decoding was effective as well as useful for lower-level reading skills. Stephanie used a concentration game from a website to give her first graders extra practice in matching beginning letter sounds to pictures. Tawanna enjoyed looking for the letter "z" when the picture of the "zebra" was revealed.

MOTIVATION

Is technology a motivation or a distraction? The answer can be found in the perception, philosophy, and implementation of technology by teachers, administrators, students, and parents. Room arrangement, extent of use, quality, and rationale all contribute to the answer to this question. For some people, technology opens up new realms of information. Carter uses videos in his room to show how sea specimens are collected and analyzed in an underwater science lab. His students are able to listen to the scientists pronounce the vocabulary words they are reading in their text. Later, his students are able to read and pronounce the terms.

Opportunities for guided practice or enrichment can be beneficial as students read with an audiotape. This can be distracting for others, though, so Lin Lei has her listening center in a corner of her room and uses headsets. Stan, a special needs child in her room, can listen to a story without distractions, thereby enabling him to understand the story and participate in later discussions with the other children. Lin Lei is careful not to have Stan spend too much time hooked up to a tape and headset because she knows how important it is for him to interact with other children.

Technology can become a distraction for some students. When students start saying "Not another video!" or, "Great—more games instead of reading," educators need to rethink the ways in which they are using technology. The bottom line for educators is: Use technology as a tool to assist instruction, not replace it. The following are descriptions of a few types of technology available and how they have been used in classrooms.

TYPES OF TECHNOLOGY

Software

Story software can help children learn how to say words, match sounds and letters or words, read with fluency, and further comprehension. Jamal listened to *Curious George Goes to the Aquarium,* by Margret and H. A. Rey, and practiced his letters and sounds while truly enjoying George's antics. He selected different pictures on each page of text and clicked on them. The computer revealed the word while saying the object. For some of the objects, Jamal knew the word—it was in his personal word bank. Other words were new to him, but he practiced associating the initial sound with the first letter of the corresponding word.

Writing software can strengthen word recognition skills as students write stories or letters or other pieces on the computer. As they write, they use their phonics understanding to spell words. In many programs when a word is misspelled, the computer alerts the writer. Children may have a chance at this point to have a go at spelling the words again (using the idea of invented or developmental spelling discussed earlier in this text).

Some programs give children a choice of words, and they apply phonics clues to decode and select the correct word. Other programs simply highlight the misspelled word until the user types it correctly. Still other programs offer the automatic correct feature so students see the computer correct a mistake as it happens. Writers receive immediate feedback on correct spellings when using word processing programs such as Microsoft Word or Works, Claris Works, and StoryBook Weaver Delux.

Teachers need to explain to students the limitations of these corrective features. Computers will not catch an error if what was mistyped is a real word but the *wrong* word. This is especially true of, but not limited to, homonyms. Also, some programs will not catch grammatical errors.

The Internet

The Internet can be useful if teachers have the time to first surf the net and find useful sites. Because the Internet comprises a huge network of resources, the potential is tremendous. With the age of information in full swing, access to a wide variety of resources is readily available. Unfortunately, as quickly as websites appear, they also disappear. Educators can use search engines to locate sites for lesson plans, activities, curriculum, authors, commercial publishers, professional organizations, and even chat rooms for educational forums.

Looking for websites on word recognition skills may stimulate ideas for teachers as they come in contact with new concepts and related links. Publishers (such as educational curriculum companies) often have websites rich with teaching ideas or resources. Related sites may offer supporting resources, such as animal or wildlife sites having animal sounds or environmental sounds. These related resources may assist emergent readers in developing phonemic awareness.

Teachers need to remind their students to be cautious about the accuracy of information they find on the Internet. Wise users can identify the source of the website and verify if the source is valid and reliable. (See Appendix G for examples of websites and software.) School pages may have age/grade-appropriate suggestions with student examples for teachers to critique.

A teacher, Samantha, found a link to a word recognition lesson plan from a third-grade teacher when she visited a Missouri public school page on which her niece had a story published. Locating and reading online journal articles, research reports, and ERIC documents may extend professional learning/development and build teachers' theoretical understanding.

Besides being supportive to teachers by providing resources, the Internet offers a tool for students. Many websites have practice activities for matching sounds, practicing spelling, and building new words, to name a few. Interactive sites for children to play word recognition games or complete activities are easily accessible. Reading activities with pupil response choices and immediate feedback encourage student learning. The challenge is to find the right site to support the classroom instruction and the students' needs.

Students often use a computer for research. Seeking information through the computer can stimulate learning because of the variety of visual and auditory presentation styles available. Students apply phonics skills when they type search terms for words they may not be able to spell. They read information on the screen that often challenges their reading level. They attend to the visual and auditory information to pick up clues for decoding words. They apply word recognition skills to understand the text on the computer. The connections to word recognition skills are limitless if teachers seek ways to incorporate the resources available on the Internet.

Videocassettes

Watching a story being read or seeing an educational "film" can support word recognition skills. Years ago on Saturday mornings, "Schoolhouse Rock" helped many children learn about rhyming words and affixes, for example. Today this same program is available on video and CD-ROM. Many commercially produced curricula are available on videocassettes. With videocassettes, teachers can extend the classroom across the world and through space. Vocabulary, for example, may be enhanced, and teachers can take advantage of students' interest in the content to practice decoding skills with their students.

Audiocassettes

Listening to books on tape can provide practice and enrichment with decoding and pronouncing words while building fluency as students read along with the storyteller. Some commercial publishers supply teachers with audiocassettes and other media that coordinate with their curriculum.

Sasha used an audiocassette that came with her basal series to assess her first graders' phonemic awareness. She had each student listen to a tape of words and match the beginning sound with the corresponding letter in the workbook. Sasha was able to determine which students needed more individual instruction after the assessment. Teachers also can use audiocassettes to record a student reading aloud or during an IRI, and play back the tape for additional analyses later.

Overhead Projectors and Filmstrips

Overhead projectors are a staple in most classrooms today. They provide a venue for large-group or small-group instruction. Teachers can copy an activity sheet for the students to do together. The overhead allows teachers or students to write directly on the sheet while everyone watches.

For example, John used an overhead with middle school students in his language arts class to reinforce decoding and pronunciation skills during dictionary use. Although filmstrips are not used as frequently as they once were, they can be beneficial in presenting word recognition skills.

Wilson (1996) described the process of creating and using stuco-slides, which may lend itself to building word recognition skills. Teachers and students can create individual stuco-slides (see Appendix H). The procedure consists of the following:

1. Develop a template for a slide on paper (2.5" × 3").
2. Edit the template carefully.
3. Affix the template within a rectangle on an outlined grid (16" × 21") that has been separated into 24 equal sections (room for 24 templates.)
4. Take the grid and templates to an offset printer (a printer who makes graduation or wedding announcements, for example) to make an 8.5" × 11" negative.
5. Cut the negative, on the grid lines evident on the negative, into individual slides and place each in a slide sleeve or jacket.
6. Color the clear lines on the slide negative with markers and assemble the slides into the proposed "show."

One application for stuco-slides for younger children is to allow them to create slides with animals or objects that have a particular initial sound. For example, three students might draw a kite, kitten, and king, respectively, for the /k/ sound. Later, the teacher could flash the slides on the wall for students to identify the term and initial sound.

For older students, developing a text with illustrations to deliver a social studies report might provide excellent reinforcement for reading and writing while offering an exciting alternative to a traditional oral report. Martin and Matthew used the stuco-slide construction to create visuals for their report on hot air ballooning. Two of Martin and Matthew's slides are illustrated. Before the artwork was sent to the printer, and as part of the writing process (editing conference with their teacher) in Mrs. Raecker's social studies class, the boys discovered that they had misspelled three words, as shown in the illustration. Mrs. Raecker reinforced the fifth graders' use of phonics generalizations to help them correct their spelling errors.

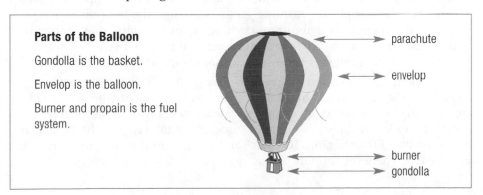

Parts of the Balloon

Gondolla is the basket.

Envelop is the balloon.

Burner and propain is the fuel system.

parachute

envelop

burner
gondolla

Laserdiscs

New audio/video tools are being developed and introduced into the field of education all the time. These afford teachers access to more information or resources in a shorter amount of time. The laserdisc is a fast and efficient mode of technology if teachers are well-trained and the equipment is readily available. With a quick scan of a bar code, a teacher or student can go to an exact clip of the information or activity selected. These are often short snippets and make immediate presentations of information. Catherine found a section on her reading series disc that related to using prefixes with words to make new words. She used it to show examples to her students and thereby vary the instruction.

STRATEGIES FOR TEACHING WITH TECHNOLOGY

Programmed instruction. Programmed instruction is a self-paced instructional program that can be individualized to meet students' specific needs. On the computer, students work through a series of prescribed exercises or questions related to a specific skill. Often mastery learning is associated with programmed instruction. In the best cases, as the student is achieving successfully, the problems become more challenging.

An example is a system in which students choose the correct spelling of words based on phonetic spellings. In programmed instruction, the words may become more difficult as the students progress, phonics generalizations they have mastered during the exercise are filtered out, and students' mastery of the generalizations practiced are assessed periodically. Educators are cautioned not to use programmed instruction as the entire reading or word recognition program. Some students may benefit from limited use.

One-computer classrooms. Teachers are often faced with the dilemma of what to do with only one computer in the classroom. Teachers have used the following activities to promote the most efficient and effective use of a computer in the classroom.

1. **Learning center.** The computer can be a designated-choice center in the room. During center time or after completing all of their work, students may choose to spend time in the computer center. Teachers can have learning games uploaded for easy access so the students can practice skills related to regular instruction. Some teachers allow students to use the computer in additional ways, such as playing learning games, searching the Internet, writing stories, sending email to epals, or researching topics through online encyclopedias. If teachers plan for center time, they may have to set a schedule for turn-taking at the computer because of its popularity with students.

2. **Individualized instruction.** Teachers may invite parents or grandparents to assist in the classroom. The adult is paired with a student who needs additional help or enrichment, allowing individual attention. This also can be done with cadet teachers (high school students volunteering in the elementary school) with a little training. Teachers can make use of the computer throughout the day, whenever support help is available.

For example, in Ruth's fourth-grade classroom, seniors from the local high school come in 2 days a week for one hour. She plans her writing process time during the cadet participation. While she and three of the cadets are having editing conferences, one cadet is working at the computer with students on word processing a final copy at the publishing stage. Another cadet is moving around the room helping other students at various stages within the writing workshop. Teachers who do not have classroom assistance may still use the computer for individualized instruction with sequenced learning software.

3. **Reward system.** Many teachers use the computer as a reward for achievement or appropriate behaviors. As a special reward, students receive time chips that they can exchange for time on the computer.

4. **Paired learning.** Using the buddy system, teachers can have two students work together at the computer. This allows more students access at the same time. Similarly, a cooperative learning group may work together at the computer.

5. **Whole-group instruction.** High-definition projectors, LCD (liquid crystal display) or similar projection equipment, and white boards can connect to the classroom computer and allow the screen image to be projected onto a screen or wall. This allows all of the students to respond visually and orally to the computer information and to their peers. Teachers also can use this approach to tap into telecommunications networks reaching other teachers and classrooms or online events or courses.

6. **Record keeping.** Teachers may take advantage of the computer in their own planning of lessons, developing instructional aids, researching information or additional resources, and even record keeping, such as grade-book programs.

Teachers have to be careful not to use the computer exclusively for one purpose in their classrooms but, rather, try to build in opportunities for use by students throughout the day. Likewise, they must not let the computer remain idle because only one computer is available. Routinely allowing students time on the classroom computer, however brief, will strengthen reading and writing while increasing their familiarity with technology. Using computer technology with today's students can be motivating, exciting, and efficient for teaching and learning.

Putting It All TOGETHER

Congress passed legislation that funded the establishment of a blue-ribbon panel to review the body of empirical research regarding how children learn to read. A news release from the National Institutes of Health on April 13, 2000, reported the findings of the National Reading Panel as "the largest, most comprehensive evidenced-based review ever conducted of research on how children learn reading" (p. 1). The report stated:

> The panel determined that effective reading instruction includes teaching children to break apart and manipulate the sounds in words (phonemic awareness), teaching them that these sounds are represented by letters of the alphabet which can then be blended together to form words (phonics), having them practice what they've learned by reading aloud with guidance and feedback (guided oral reading), and applying reading comprehension strategies to guide and improve reading comprehension. (p. 1)

Throughout this book we have attempted to address these important issues through definitions, explanations, and suggested teaching strategies. In this final section of the

book, we attempt to show how all the pieces of the puzzle fit together to enable comprehension. Readers who have effective word recognition skills can put together words,
sentences, and punctuation more quickly, resulting in fluent reading. Comprehension, the
ultimate goal in reading, can be strengthened with specific word recognition strategies.
Because the reading–writing connection is so strong, teachers can involve their students
daily in meaningful writing activities to help them build reading skills. Teachers can integrate
word recognition across the curriculum to show students how knowledge of these reading
skills will help them in everything they do. Finally, this section covers state and national standards, professional organizations, professional development, collaboration, and reflection.

Developing Fluency

Fluency, according to Harris and Sipay (1990), is present when "word
recognition is rapid and accurate, the words are grouped in thought units
(phrased acceptably), reading flows smoothly, and the voice is used to
indicate an acceptable understanding of the text" (p. 209). Fluency comes when
readers are quickly able to recognize words so reading is smooth and uninter-
rupted. A student who is not fluent in reading still may have word recognition
problems. This can lead to problems with comprehension as well. If a reader
struggles over many words, the thought or meaning of the sentence can get lost
because the reader is working more on word recognition than comprehension.

In a presentation titled "Fluency Oriented Reading Instruction" at the Center
for the Improvement of Early Reading Achievement Institute, Stahl (2000) stated, "The most important thing we can do to improve children's reading
achievement is to have them read as much connected text at their instructional
level as possible." The best way to develop fluency in reading is through practice
in reading. Some strategies to help students develop fluency follow.

STRATEGIES TO DEVELOP FLUENCY

CLUSTERING

ALL

When students have problems with adequate phrasing, teachers can use the
clustering technique, in which readers combine two to four words and train
their eyes to see all the words in a cluster at a glance.

1. Find a short passage and discuss how some words seem to go together.
2. Circle groups of words, as shown in the example below.
3. Discuss how clustering words in meaningful groupings promotes fluent
   reading.

This strategy is particularly helpful with students who are reading but not
rapidly with comprehension. ESL students who can decode words but who have
not achieved smooth fluency also will benefit. Learning to see words in clusters
can help students with fluency, and therefore comprehension.

(My dad and I) (are going) (to the fair tomorrow.)

CHORAL READING

Choral reading—reading aloud in unison or in turn—is an effective tool to help students build fluency. Some parts of a story or book can be read by the entire class, and others are assigned to one or more readers. One good book to use for choral reading is *Is Your Mama a Llama,* by Deborah Guarino. The class can be divided in half. One half reads the dialogue, and the other half reads the rest. So the first side reads, "Is your mama a llama?" and the other side reads, "I asked my friend Rhonda." The first side reads, "'No, she is not,'" then the second side follows with, "is how Rhonda responded." This continues throughout the book. *Chicka Chicka Boom Boom,* by Bill Martin, Jr. and John Archambault, is a fun book for a class to read aloud in unison. With this activity, teachers can model fluent reading and allow students to practice reading with expression.

PRIMARY
INTERMEDIATE

Choral reading is also an effective way for a reading group to share poetry with the rest of the class. After some experience with teacher-directed pieces, students probably will be ready to handle some of their own arranging and directing. Having students select and plan a choral reading for a class presentation or for audiotaping or videotaping provides an excellent class activity. Choral reading is also a good way to "show off" students' reading ability at a Parent-Teacher-Student Association meeting.

VARIATION. In Mr. Whitmore's history class, he had his students divide the Declaration of Independence into parts for students to choral read. He found this to be an effective way for the students to practice reading important documents from history and helped them remember these documents better through practice, repetition, and hearing the text orally.

INTERMEDIATE
MIDDLE
SECONDARY
ESL

DUET READING

In **duet reading,** the teacher and a student together or an experienced reader and a struggling reader read a selection together. More experienced readers read at normal speed, using expression and following the punctuation. Less experienced readers read along moving their finger under the line they are reading. After a few sessions, the inexperienced reader will have an easier time keeping up.

PRIMARY
INTERMEDIATE
ESL

ECHO READING

In **echo reading,** an experienced reader first reads a phrase or two and the less experienced reader immediately repeats what was read. This helps the inexperienced reader hear the phrase read correctly and fluently before reading it independently.

PRIMARY
INTERMEDIATE
ESL

REPEATED READINGS

An effective way for students to practice fluency is through repeated reading of a passage. Students can choose a short passage to read over and over until they know all the words and punctuation so they can read quickly and easily.

ALL

Students can practice reading silently or orally. A more formal method of repeated readings is to have the teacher choose 100 words for students to read and time their reading while marking errors. Students reread the passage until they can read it with 0 or 1 error and can read at a rate of 100 words per minute.

INTERMEDIATE
MIDDLE
SECONDARY
ESL

VARIATION. In content-area classrooms, teachers often have students take turns reading aloud from the text. Teachers can allow students to choose a selection or can assign specific paragraphs for the students to read ahead of time so they have an opportunity to practice reading before reading aloud in front of their peers. Repeated readings give reluctant readers more confidence in addition to the boost in fluency and comprehension.

RECREATIONAL READING

ALL

The best way to improve at anything is to practice, and one of the best ways to practice reading is by reading books for enjoyment. Encourage students to read easy, interesting books for pleasure at or near the students' independent reading level. Students at all grade levels in all subjects should be encouraged to read for enjoyment. To help students find books on their reading level, teachers can remind students of Veatch's (1966) "rule of thumb" (see page 5 for the "rule").

Comprehension Building

As the title of Unit 4 indicates, at some point students must put all the word recognition skills together and apply them to their reading. Most readers, teachers, and education authorities agree that comprehension, or understanding of text, is the ultimate goal of reading. The purpose of teachers' teaching the skills and students' learning the skills is to create independent readers—readers who can approach a chosen text with confidence, choose to read for recreation, and know what to do when they come upon a word they do not know.

Even though each word recognition skill can be defined, discussed, and taught somewhat independently, comprehension is not a set of discrete skills. Rather, it is a blend of all word recognition skills, a seamless process in which skilled reading flows from one word recognition skill to another. In using word recognition skills, it is difficult to isolate one skill from another. Comprehension involves word recognition, fluency, prior knowledge, and interacting with text. All these things work together to help readers understand what they are reading.

Besides the word recognition skills of phonics, structural analysis, context clues involving semantics and syntax, sight words, and vocabulary, two related components of reading comprehension warrant consideration: (1) prior knowledge about the selected topic, and (2) attitude toward reading in general. These skills cannot be taught. Rather, they are an accumulation of students' experiences with life.

Teachers must recognize the importance of prior knowledge in learning to read with comprehension, find ways to activate or call up that store of knowledge, and also find ways to connect the familiar, known information to the new and unknown. Smith (1998a) puts it this way: "Understanding means you are connecting what is new to what you know already" (p. 88). Relating the new to the known fits well with metacognitive and schema theory that comprehension is a complex interactive process in which readers play an active-constructive role in bringing meaning to text.

Often, students merely need to be prompted to remember what they already know about a topic, such as concepts or vocabulary words. For example, 8-year-old Jared loves dinosaurs and knows that some dinosaurs were plant-eating and some were meat-eating. Jared would easily learn the science vocabulary words "herbivorous" and "carnivorous" because he knows what the two terms mean.

Because Jared loves dinosaurs, he already has a positive attitude about learning more information on this topic. His teacher's challenge is to maintain that enthusiasm as the lessons extend to other extinct animals and what caused their demise. If integrated thematic units are used, this positive attitude could be extended to content areas besides science, such as social studies, math, and language arts. Jared most likely would want to read about dinosaurs during recreational reading time at school and at home, sharing books with his parents.

Even though Jared has both prior knowledge about many topics and a positive attitude about reading, his teacher wants to continually make sure that textbook material and information books in the classroom are at his reading level. She may decide to give him an informal reading inventory to identify his reading levels, to discover his word recognition skills in oral reading, to determine his comprehension level, and to detect his vocabulary development. With this information in hand, she can better plan for instruction to meet Jared's specific needs.

Effective teachers know that as readers comprehend the meaning of text, they do so at several levels of understanding or complexity. Readers would be helped by being aware that they can strengthen their reading comprehension at the literal level (understanding and retaining information stated directly in the reading material), at the inferential level (understanding and applying concepts not directly stated but implied), and at the evaluative level (understanding concepts and making critical judgments about accuracy, acceptability, value, or other factors). Several strategies that teachers can use to help strengthen students' comprehension, concentration, motivation, and attitude toward reading are given next.

STRATEGIES TO BUILD COMPREHENSION

THE THREE P'S

The three P's in this strategy stand for *purpose, prediction,* and *prior knowledge* (Tonjes & Zintz, 1981). Teachers can model this strategy.

1. Determine a *purpose.* Teachers can model how to set a purpose or reason for reading by using a think-aloud.
2. *Predict* what might happen based on the book title, illustrations, and chapter titles.
3. Connect their life experiences to the prediction and purpose by calling up *prior knowledge.*

4. Discuss how the three P's help students' comprehension, and encourage independent use of the strategy.

Mr. Messina asked his students to read the first chapter of *Ramona's World,* by Beverly Cleary, to find out what good news Ramona wanted to share. He continued by asking students to look at the cover of the book and skim the illustrations inside the book to predict what the whole book was about. If students were familiar with the Ramona character from Cleary's earlier books, they could activate their prior knowledge to predict what might occur in this new book. Mr. Messina reminded them to think about events in previous books, thereby connecting prior knowledge to prediction.

As teachers model this strategy, students are encouraged to do these steps with each reading selection they encounter. Ideally, students begin to do this on their own without teacher prompting. Word recognition skills are enhanced as success in reading and fluency develop as a result of preparing for the text.

MIDDLE
SECONDARY
ESL

VARIATION. In Mr. MacGrail's history class, he had students use the three P's before reading a chapter on slavery in the Civil War. Students asked themselves what their purpose was in reading the chapter. They each predicted what might be included in the chapter and they called on their prior knowledge about blacks being persecuted plus their own feelings when they have been forced to do something against their own will.

DIRECTED READING–THINKING ACTIVITY (DR–TA)

INTERMEDIATE
MIDDLE
SECONDARY
ESL

The **directed reading–thinking activity (DR–TA),** conceived by Stauffer (1969), directs students' predicting and thinking as they read, thereby strengthening their comprehension of the text. During this activity, teachers separate a reading selection (expository or narrative) into sections. If possible, the pauses should be at a suspense point in a narrative, or at an obvious stopping point in expository text. At each stopping point, students make predictions that encourage divergent thinking about the rest of the selection. The teacher begins by asking students to read to themselves the title of a selection. Then the teacher asks the following three open-ended questions:

1. What do you think will happen?
2. Why do you think so?
3. Are there any other possibilities?

After discussion, the teacher asks the students to read silently to another point in the story, and repeats the same three questions. The reading and predicting continue until the end of the story. The teacher responds neutrally and accepts all answers. DR–TAs can be helpful for teachers in pulling out new vocabulary during questions and answers. Teachers also can support word recognition skills such as context clues as students describe reasons for their answers to the questions posed.

For more mature readers, short stories by O. Henry, such as "Hearts and Hands" and "After Twenty Years," work well with this strategy because of his surprise endings. The DR–TA strategy helps students better understand what they are reading by making them more aware of the text as they read and as they hear other students' predictions.

GUIDED READING PROCEDURE

ALL

The **guided reading procedure (GRP)**, developed by Manzo (1975), is a technique students can use to recall details and help organize information (not to be confused with "guided reading" by Fountas and Pinnell). Teachers can follow these steps:

1. Have students read a passage after being told to remember everything they can.
2. Have students brainstorm with the teacher everything they can remember from the passage, with their books closed. List everything on the chalkboard or overhead transparency.
3. Ask students to go back to the text and correct or add to the list any information not remembered.
4. Direct the class or small groups in organizing the list of information into some meaningful order. Often, webbing or mapping—a visual kind of outlining—is helpful in organizing the information.
5. Discuss with the class how the listing and organization of information aided their comprehension.

A similar strategy based on the GRP, activating prior knowledge, was used with middle school and secondary students preparing to study about Abraham Lincoln (Hurst, 2000). Before reading, students were asked to list as much as they knew about Lincoln while the teacher wrote the facts on the board using a semantic web format. In a semantic web, the main subject is written in a circle in the center of the chalkboard. Each fact that is given is separated according to topics, then the subtopics are linked as in Figure 4.1.

VARIATION. Next the class was divided into groups of three to four and provided with a text to read about Lincoln. After reading the text together, each group came to the board and added new facts they learned from the text. The groups wrote a moral or one-sentence lesson to the story based on what they read, and

INTERMEDIATE

MIDDLE

SECONDARY

ESL

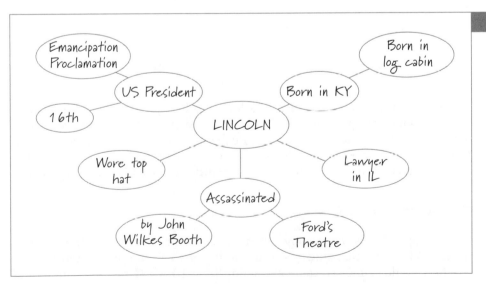

FIGURE 4.1

Sample semantic web format using Abraham Lincoln.

taped the paper to the board. After each group had completed these assignments, the teacher had each group share the new facts they had added, read their moral or lesson, and explain the moral or lesson.

RADIO READING

INTERMEDIATE
MIDDLE
SECONDARY
ESL

Radio reading (Searfoss, 1975) provides a highly motivating alternative to round-robin reading.

1. Organize students into groups of three to five.
2. Divide a text into three to five sections prior to the activity.
3. Assign a section to each student within each group.
4. Have students begin by reading their own section silently and compose one question for each other member of their group based on the information in their section.
5. Have each student read aloud his or her section like a radio announcer while the other group members listen without looking at the passage.
6. Have the reader ask each member of the group a question to prompt discussion.
7. Give each student in the group a turn at reading and questioning.

This activity strengthens listening, comprehension, oral reading, and question-constructing skills. It also supports word recognition skills related to phonics as readers hear each other pronounce words.

REQUEST

INTERMEDIATE
MIDDLE
SECONDARY
ESL

ReQuest (Manzo, 1969) helps students strengthen their silent reading comprehension.

1. The teacher and students silently read a section of text.
2. Students question the teacher about the passage.
3. Roles are exchanged.
4. The teacher questions the students about the passage.
5. The sequence of read and question is repeated several times until the teacher asks the students to make predictions about the rest of the text.
6. The students read the rest of the text silently.

In a variation, students begin to ask each other questions after the first or second round of questions. ReQuest helps silent reading comprehension through the use of questioning. It is valuable for teachers to identify the word recognition strategies that students use during silent reading if teachers plan questions related to uncovering unknown words or vocabulary development.

RECREATIONAL READING

ALL

Students at all levels will become better readers if they are allowed time in class to read. The more that students read, the better their comprehension will be. Teachers could name recreational reading time DEAR (Drop Everything and

Read), SSR (Sustained Silent Reading), or something similar. The important thing is that students have opportunities to read every day. Recreational reading should not be limited to elementary classrooms.

Incorporating Multiple Intelligences

Many factors contribute to the decisions teachers make about instruction and learning. Teachers must stay abreast of current trends and issues in education so they can change or modify their practices when needed. They should be cautious, however, and not try to incorporate everything that comes along. Being an effective teacher requires reflective decision making based on the needs of the students and the teacher. An area of increasing research that teachers should consider is Gardner's (1983) *multiple intelligences (MI)* theory. Teachers can implement word recognition practice while reinforcing Gardner's theory by applying MI concepts in their lesson planning. MI theory suggests that intelligence should be defined or measured through multiple ways. Human beings possess intelligences or "smarts" in eight areas, some of which are stronger than others. Gardner and others (Armstrong, 1994; Gardner, 1983) have shown that when learning new material, students who use one or more of their stronger intelligences will increase their learning or assimilate knowledge more readily. Encountering new material using a comfortable intelligence assists students in creating connections to prior knowledge and building confidence.

Familiarity with the eight intelligences will help teachers plan for student practice of word recognition skills using the children's various intelligences, and thereby meet their needs more successfully. The eight areas are: verbal/linguistic, mathematical/logical, visual/spatial, bodily/kinesthetic, musical/rhythmic, interpersonal, intrapersonal, and naturalistic. A brief description of each, along with some teaching applications, follows.

VERBAL/LINGUISTIC

Students who are "word-smart" (Armstrong, 1994, p. 39) are adept in verbal skills and often think in words. They enjoy reading, playing word games, talking, writing, storytelling, and vocabulary building. Word recognition skills intrigue word-smart students by giving additional strategies for uncovering new words and meanings. To reinforce word recognition skills, have students:

1. Write poetry or read frequently to rehearse syntax and semantic cluing strategies.
2. Read aloud to emphasize fluency in using the skills.
3. Complete word problems to practice phonics, writing, and vocabulary development in content areas.
4. Correspond with pen pals, by letter or email message, to reinforce the writing influence on word recognition skills.
5. Listen to books on tape to support phonics and phonemic awareness.
6. Be a storyteller to fortify use of phonics in oral communication.
7. Read the newspaper to apply strategies for decoding unfamiliar words.

8. Look up words to strengthen dictionary use in word recognition.
9. Play 20 questions to acquire context clues skills.

MATHEMATICAL/LOGICAL

Students who are "number-smart" (Armstrong, 1994, p. 39) see patterns and relationships in numbers and concepts. They like to solve problems, work with numbers, use formulas and patterns, make outlines, and play logic games. To reinforce word recognition skill:

1. Create a timeline showing when to use word recognition skills.
2. Make a graph of how frequently students use each strategy in their independent reading.
3. Classify objects to demonstrate phonemic awareness of beginning sounds or other criteria.
4. Do a brainteaser, posing a word recognition skill that students are to identify.
5. Create an outline of steps in using a word recognition skill or supporting skill such as dictionary use.
6. Experiment with word building to develop new words.

VISUAL/SPATIAL

Students who are "picture-smart" (Armstrong, 1994, p. 39) think in images and pictures; they are aware of objects, shapes, colors, and patterns. They like to draw, paint, make designs and patterns, do puzzles, and visualize (using the mind's eye). To reinforce word recognition skills, have students:

1. Put together a word puzzle using the letters of a vocabulary term to build phonics.
2. Daydream about a place and describe it using adjectives to reinforce semantic clues.
3. Play a board game with directions that use new terms, to assist in syntax.
4. Build a mystery box with things that use a given letter, to practice phonemic awareness.
5. Make a diorama and place labels on it, to develop sight words.
6. Draw a map using key terms to strengthen vocabulary.
7. Paint a picture that tells a story to connect oral communication and visual clues.

BODILY/KINESTHETIC

Students who are "body-smart" (Armstrong, 1994, p. 39) have a keen sense of their body and physical movement, are coordinated, and enjoy physically expressing themselves. They like movement, dance, role-playing, dramatics, playing physical games, and hands-on projects. They prefer to be active in the learning process. To reinforce word recognition skills, have students:

1. Pantomime or play charades for a word or phrase, to reinforce structural analysis or word parts.

2. Act out a scene from a story to build on visual clues.
3. Learn sign language to develop vocabulary.
4. Put actions to a story to strengthen context or visual clues.
5. Create puppet shows to assist in vocabulary building.
6. Go on a scavenger hunt to augment phonemic awareness.
7. Use manipulatives for kinesthetic learners to assist in seeing the words as they are classified or matching sounds with symbols.

MUSICAL/RHYTHMIC

Students who are "music-smart" (Armstrong, 1994, p. 39) are sensitive to music, sounds, and rhythmic patterns. They notice and sense various sounds, tones, and beats. They learn through music, environmental sounds, singing, rapping, playing instruments, and rhyming. To reinforce word recognition skills, have students:

1. Add sound effects to a story to support phonemic awareness.
2. Make up a cheer to reinforce semantics.
3. Play "Name that Tune" to observe sound identifications.
4. Tap out a rhythm to practice syllabication or structural analysis.
5. Sing or put to music a nursery rhyme to build semantic or syntax skills.
6. Make a song to help students remember information that connects vocabulary to meaning.

INTERPERSONAL

Students who are "people-smart" (Armstrong, 1994, p. 39) learn best through person-to-person interactions. Friendships and socialization are natural and important to these children. Cooperative learning situations and group activities are pleasurable for them. They are sensitive to others, relate well to peers, and are good at conflict resolution. To reinforce word recognition skills, have students:

1. Write a story with a partner to broaden vocabulary and practice phonics through writing.
2. Solve a dispute to enhance oral language skills and the use of context.
3. Engage in buddy reading to model phonics and general word recognition skills.
4. Read, work, and cooperate with others to increase fluency and knowledge of the English language.
5. Play a game with a friend to reinforce oral language and decoding strategies when reading rules or cards are involved.
6. Participate in class discussions to support vocabulary development, phonemic awareness, and all the word recognition skills.

INTRAPERSONAL

Students who are "self-smart" (Armstrong, 1994, p. 39) are self-aware and reflective. They are in tune with their inner feelings and have insight and understanding about themselves. They often prefer to work alone and enjoy quiet writing and reading. They tend to concentrate on what they are doing, excluding outside factors, and prefer thought-provoking activities. To reinforce word recognition skills, have students:

1. Write an autobiography, applying word recognition skills.
2. Keep a diary, using decoding and phonics strategies for developmental spelling.
3. Reflect on what is learned to strengthen self-understanding of how fluency develops, attitudes toward reading, and how word recognition skills are used.
4. Create a poem to increase personal vocabulary.
5. Engage in independent study to develop lifelong reading habits.

NATURALISTIC

Students who are "nature-smart" are in touch with nature and their natural surroundings. They enjoy being outdoors and working with living things. They are energized by the sun and take notice of changes in the weather and seasons. To reinforce word recognition skills, have students:

1. Participate in field studies to strengthen word recognition skills through writing.
2. Take observation notes to build structural analysis through word building.
3. Participate in outdoor classrooms to increase vocabulary.
4. Make sand drawings to practice letter-sound relationships from dictated words.
5. Go on scavenger hunts to enhance phonemic awareness by looking for nature sounds.
6. Explore the outdoors to broaden contextual word analysis.

Best practices in working with multiple intelligences call for varied experiences in all of the areas, not simply those that are students' weakest or strongest, but teachers should not try to incorporate all eight areas in every lesson. Giving additional practice periodically through one or more of the multiple intelligences will help reach students who perceive information through different learning styles or smarts.

Connecting Reading, Writing, and Spelling

Research has shown that reading and writing are closely related. Clay (1991) states that reading and writing are complementary. As a rule, when children are engaged in both reading and writing, as one is strengthened, so is the other. When children are first learning to write, they rely on their knowledge of phonics to invent spellings for words they are using (sometimes called developmental spelling). Young children begin writing with pictures or symbols to represent sounds and move to conventional letters as they make the sound–letter connection. They begin with one letter signifying a word, such as "b" for *basketball*. As they come to better understand the sound–letter relationship and the reading and writing process, they stretch their invented spellings to multiple sounds and letters. They might write "crkus" for "circus." They hear sounds and match those sounds to letters they think make those sounds.

Gentry (1997) tells parents in his book, *My Kid Can't Spell!*, "Spelling opens the gateways to literacy by helping your child meet the requirements for beginning reading: (1) breaking the code of the alphabet, and (2) learning about sounds in words" (p. 1). Gentry further explains that "knowledge of the alphabet and the awareness that sounds make words actually predict success with reading" (p. 2) and that "spelling provides clearly discernible guideposts along your child's journey to literacy" (p. 1). Teachers can watch their students' reading and word recognition skills grow and expand as they watch their spelling and writing evolve. Spelling and reading are two sides of the same coin. Spelling is the mirror of decoding; it is *encoding*. By looking at how children spell, teachers can tell what students know about vowels, consonants, blends, and how letters work together to form sounds. How children spell shows teachers how students think about letters and words and reading.

Harris and Hodges (1995) state, "The writing approach to reading stresses meaning over grapheme–phoneme correspondences and interprets invented spellings as attempts by the student to understand the code system" (pp. 284–285). In Harste's (1989) *New Policy Guidelines for Reading*, he emphasizes that reading and writing work together to improve reading comprehension. He states, for example, "Effective teachers of reading create classroom environments in which children actively use reading and writing as tools for learning. . . . Good language arts programs highlight reading and writing . . . [and] teachers should set up functional reading and writing environments" (pp. 49–50). Harste does not separate the skills of reading and writing. In her study, Stotsky (1983) found that better readers tend to make better writers and better writers are better readers. Therefore, encouraging children to write and providing them opportunities to write every day is part of helping them grow as readers. According to Calkins (1986), "If we teach children the power of writing to learn across the curriculum, we will also teach them the power of writing—and of thinking—across their lives" (p. 498). Writing also fosters development of word recognition skills in addition to phonics.

Writing can help students develop additional vocabulary. In composing a story, a student may seek a new word to describe an observation or characteristic. MacKenzie was writing her own version of *The Very Hungry Caterpillar*, by Eric Carle, and decided that her caterpillar ate "3 graps and 4 skashs, and 5 Ress pecs" for "three grapes and four squashes and five Reeses Pieces." In this example, the teacher could see several word recognition skills emerging: numbers representing concepts (semantics), words made into plurals using "s" (structural analysis), adjectives and nouns placed together to develop the meaning (syntax), and phonemic awareness leading to developmental spelling (phonics). Also evident is the student's vocabulary and background, with the choice of squash as a food for the hungry caterpillar to eat. Teachers can learn a great deal from analyzing children's writing and spelling.

STRATEGIES TO CONNECT READING AND WRITING

ALL

LETTER WRITING

Letter writing is a great way for students to practice reading and writing. Teachers can write to their students and encourage students to write back. Although teachers' editing or correcting students' writing on an activity such as this usually is not a good idea, teachers can make notes to themselves about the types of student errors they notice so teachers can plan minilessons on those skills/strategies. Students can write to each other, as well as to parents, pen pals, students in other classes, and friends. Email is an excellent way for students to interact with others through writing. Students at all grade levels can benefit from this activity.

LANGUAGE EXPERIENCE APPROACH ACTIVITIES

PRIMARY
INTERMEDIATE

Activities in the **language experience approach** can be used to provide text for instructional work related to increasing sight vocabulary, word recognition skills, and review of comprehension skills. For a language experience activity, the student or students are asked to dictate a story while the teacher prints it word for word. The teacher points to each word as the student(s) reads the story aloud. The following day, the student(s) and teacher read the story aloud together and the teacher points to each word as they read it. When working with an individual, the teacher asks the student to underline words that he or she recognizes. The words are put on cards.

When the student recognizes the words in isolation on 2 consecutive days, the words go into a word bank. The student and the teacher read the story aloud daily until the student feels comfortable reading the story aloud by himself or herself. In working with a class or a small group, the words from the story may become the focus for additional instruction.

INTERMEDIATE
MIDDLE
SECONDARY
ESL

VARIATION. For older students who read at a level far below their grade, finding reading material at their interest level sometimes is difficult. These students might tell the teacher or tutor a story about something they have done, such as playing in a football game or attending a concert. The teacher types the story for the students to read. The teacher then asks the students to edit their stories or add new material. Every word in the story will have come from the students' speaking vocabulary.

READING/WRITING WORKSHOP

INTERMEDIATE
MIDDLE
SECONDARY
ESL

Teachers can set up reading and writing time in a workshop format. In her book *In the Middle,* Atwell (1987) describes the reading/writing workshop she used with her students. At the beginning of each class period, she presented a minilesson on a skill that students might work on that day, then modeled that skill. The students wrote independently, incorporating that new skill as they wrote. Atwell circulated around the room, working with individual students. She also held group conferences in which she worked with several students at once. Finally, she gave the students opportunities to share their work with the entire class. On reading days, the students responded to her through a letter in a literature log about what they were reading, and she responded to them about her own reading.

Using this model, students receive many and varied opportunities to read and write with instruction, modeling, guidance, and encouragement. The reading/writing workshop helps students improve their reading by having time for writing. The minilesson format allows teachers to focus on specific word recognition skills as needed.

JOURNALS

Journals can be structured in several ways. Dialog journals generally are intended for students to engage in a back-and-forth discourse with their teachers. Buddy journals are a means for students to interact with each other. In reading journals, students respond to what they are reading.

STRATEGIES TO CONNECT READING AND SPELLING

FINGER-TRACING

PRIMARY

Encouraging students to trace over words with their finger helps them remember the words better. Second-grade teacher Kate Companik has her students spray shaving lotion on their desks and then write their spelling words in the foam. Children love this tactile activity.

SPARKLE

PRIMARY
INTERMEDIATE
MIDDLE

Second-grade teacher Jane Hokanson finds success with the spelling game Sparkle.

1. Have students stand in a circle facing each other.
2. Say a spelling word.
3. The first student says the first letter of the word.
4. The next person says the next letter and so on until the last letter of the word has been said.
5. After the last letter has been said, the next person in line says, "Sparkle!"
6. Then the next person sits down.
7. The game continues until only one student is left.

This game helps students practice spelling words in a fun way and gives equal advantages to all students.

SCRABBLE AND BOGGLE

A wonderful way for students to practice spelling is by playing games such as Scrabble and Boggle, in which making words and spelling them correctly is the game's main purpose. Students work on their spelling skills without even realizing it.

GENERALIZATION CHARTS

INTERMEDIATE
MIDDLE
SECONDARY
ESL

Have students create a chart of spelling generalizations that they can refer to when writing either individually or as class. Students may add words to the chart as they encounter new generalizations. A separate column may be added for exceptions to the generalizations, as in the example below.

SPELLING GENERALIZATIONS	EXAMPLES	EXCEPTIONS
"i before e except after c"	believe receive	neighbor weigh
"u always follows q"	quiet quack	Iraq
"change y to an i"	candies happiest	boys days

Integrating Word Recognition Across the Curriculum

Word recognition skills can be taught and reinforced in every subject, not just during reading time. Any time a student comes to an unknown word in any subject, a teacher can stop and talk to the student about how to figure out that word and help the student make connections to the word. For example, a few years ago when the television cartoon show "Power Rangers" was at its height of popularity among children, one teacher used the children's knowledge of the show to teach a word in science. The fourth-grade students were being introduced to the concept of metamorphosis. The teacher knew that when the five teenagers on the show shouted "Morphin' time," that meant it was time for them to *change* into the Power Rangers. When the call came to "morph," they "changed." When the teacher looked at part of the word and explained it, the students were able to remember that metamorphosis has to do with change and they were more apt to understand and remember the process of metamorphosis.

The terminology and jargon of various subject areas can be complex. New vocabulary can be analyzed and figured out using word recognition skills. Following are some ways by which word recognition skills can be incorporated throughout the curriculum.

STRATEGIES TO INTEGRATE WORD RECOGNITION

ALPHALISTS

ALL

After reading a passage from a content-area text such as science or social studies, have students write the alphabet vertically down the left side of a piece of paper. After each letter, have the students write a word or words they used or learned from the text starting with each letter. For example, after reading about insects and spiders, students in Ms. Walla's class wrote: "A—arachnid, B—bugs, C—caterpillar" and so on. AlphaLists can be made individually, in groups, or as a whole class. In Mr. Reold's geography class, one group's list began: "A— Austria, B—Brazil, C—Canada." AlphaLists help students think back about what they just read and important words from the text.

CONTENT WORD WALLS

INTERMEDIATE
MIDDLE
SECONDARY
ESL

Again, a word wall is a good place to display common or important words that students need to know and remember. Word walls also are effective for content-specific terminology. Each subject area has words related to the field that students need to know to understand what they are reading. Teachers can create content word walls as they begin a new unit of study. For example, before Mr. Zane started a study of the Revolutionary War, he covered a bulletin board in his room with white paper. He had students tell everything they already knew about the war and wrote it in a web on the paper. As students learned new information during the unit, they came to the wall and added it to the web.

A variation is to write categories across the top of the bulletin board. For example, categories for the American Revolution might be people, events, locations, dates, and vocabulary. As students learn about things such as the Boston Tea Party, they go to the board and add it under the "events" category, or add "indentured servants" to "vocabulary." Students also can add the new words in a special glossary they create to go with the unit of study.

SKETCH TO STRETCH

ALL

In an activity called sketch to stretch (Harste, Short, & Burke, 1988), students who are visual learners can make a quick sketch of new words or text to help them visualize or remember the words.

1. Place students in groups of four or five.
2. Have students read a provided text.
3. Direct the discussion of the text within the groups, and have individuals or the group as a whole construct a sketch that relates to the text.
4. Have individuals or the group share the drawing and ask classmates to predict what is intended.
5. Have the artists share their interpretation of the picture.

For example, students reading about animals might focus on the terms *carnivore, herbivore,* and *omnivore.* They could sketch a picture of an animal head with large fangs for carnivore, an animal head with a plant beside it for herbivore, and a combination of both for omnivore.

As another example, in Mr. Spiegel's history class, he put the students into groups and had each group make a simple drawing of each of the Bill of Rights. The groups each shared their sketches with the rest of the class and explained why they chose to draw what they did.

ALL

Integrating the word recognition skill of structural analysis works well in content-area subjects. When Ms. Wright taught her math students the geometry terms *pentagon, hexagon, octagon,* and *decagon,* she explained what the word parts mean. By teaching students that "gon" means angles, "penta" means five, "hexa" means six, "octa" means eight, and "deca" means 10, they can better understand and remember what the shapes look like.

Teaching Responsibly

Educators are challenged more than ever to meet the needs of a wide diversity of learners in school. In this age of information, societal changes have placed teachers in the position of preparing young people to take their place in workforces armed with skills in problem solving, application of knowledge, interpersonal communications, and literacy. Accountability has become a public expectation rather than a desire. Policymakers are calling for strict standards based upon competencies for preservice teacher educators as well as inservice educators. Consequently, part of being a responsible teacher is not only to provide the best environment for students to learn and achieve in school but also to develop certain professional attributes.

Effective educators base their philosophy and teaching procedures on national, state, and local standards and competencies, using them as guideposts. They seek opportunities to constantly learn new instructional practices through professional development opportunities and collaboration with colleagues. They reflect routinely upon their methodology and goals. These areas are among those that contribute to professionalism.

KNOWLEDGE OF STANDARDS

With the attention to excellence in education and the national focus on academic achievement, broad standards or frameworks have been established at national and state levels. At district and school levels, the standards are more detailed. Professional organizations have had input in writing the standards. An example of a national standard impacting the area of word recognition is Standard 3 from the IRA/NCTE Standards for the English Language Arts:

> Students apply a wide range of strategies to comprehend, interpret, evaluate, and appreciate texts. They draw on their prior experience, their interactions with other readers and writers, their knowledge of word meaning and of other texts, their word identification strategies, and their understanding of textual features (e.g., sound letter correspondence, sentence structure, content, graphics). (p. 3)

Within this standard, the explicit notation of word recognition skills informs teachers that this is an area that students must have mastered for students at the time of graduation. These skills are taught across grade levels, built upon each year with more complex texts, and within all content areas. The above goal attaches word recognition skills to students' abilities to understand texts and use higher-level thinking, in addition to reading for appreciation, not exclusively for information. IRA/NCTE believes that good readers must be able to apply word recognition skills to derive meaning during independent reading for any purpose.

The national and state frameworks set the broad picture for the standards, and local or district standards often itemize the specific skills and knowledge that students must have at the different grade levels. Teachers should obtain both the state and the local standards to use as a planning resource in developing the scope and sequence for the coming school year. The local competencies should be the goals underpinning the units and lessons taught, to ensure that teachers and students cover the necessary concepts and skills.

PROFESSIONAL DEVELOPMENT

Professional development requires taking responsibility for ongoing learning. For teachers, that may mean obtaining continuing education credits at a university, participating in workshops or inservice opportunities, and attending conferences. Reading research studies and educational journals and participating in learned societies and professional organizations also strengthen educators' knowledge base.

Teachers do have some choice in required professional development activities, and professional development should not be limited to mandatory training. Becoming consumers of educational research can expand teachers' understanding of best practices and provide new learning theories. Reading professional publications regularly helps to stay current with the issues and trends. Often, teacher practitioner ideas are included in special sections of journals. Additional resources—book titles, articles and documents, websites, and software connected to word recognition but not used specifically in the writing of this textbook—are provided at the end of this text to assist teachers in growing professionally.

Another good way for teachers to keep abreast with new ideas and to grow as teachers is to participate in teacher study groups. A teacher study group is "a collaborative group organized and sustained by teachers to help them strengthen their professional development in areas of common interest" (Cramer, Hurst, & Wilson, 1996, p. 7). In these groups, teachers are in charge of their own independent learning while seeking personal goals through interaction with others. A teacher study group, for instance, might choose to work with word recognition skills.

COLLABORATION WITH COLLEAGUES

In shaping their professional growth as teachers, collaborating with other teachers is important. Short, Giorgis, and Pritchard (1993) found that "educators need to work with each other to think, analyze, and create conditions for change within their specific circumstances that relate to their personal or professional needs" (p. 3). Bullough and Gitlin (1991) believe that teachers need to be a community of learners supporting and sustaining each others' growth.

For example, a teacher can observe another teacher's lesson that focuses on word recognition skills or ask veteran teachers how they build word recognition skills. Teachers must take the initiative to seek out resources that will help them become better teachers. August, a first-year, fifth-grade teacher, was enjoying her communication arts block in the morning—with the exception of recreational reading time. While she was taught in her university reading courses to set aside a few minutes every day for students to read independently, and she was to model free reading and read herself, she often felt cheated out of the reading time. Her students frequently came up and asked her to tell them what a particular word was. She found herself spending her reading time answering questions.

One afternoon she talked with Elaine, a veteran teacher in the room next to her. August asked Elaine if she was having difficulty with students' questions during DEAR (drop everything and read) time. Elaine replied that she had trained her students to "try three ways" (use three word recognition strategies) before they could ask for help. Elaine had spent two class periods reviewing skills the students already knew, such as decoding sounds, looking for context clues, and sometimes referring to the dictionary. She modeled, through think-alouds, how she used the skills when she read. At first her students had tried to get by, saying that they had tried everything, but Elaine asked the students to tell her the strategies they had attempted. Her students quickly learned to "try three ways" before they came to her. Elaine explained to August that her students rarely came to her for help now, and they were becoming stronger independent readers because they were using their word recognition skills routinely during reading.

REFLECTION

Reflection is a powerful attribute in teachers—stopping to rethink a lesson, critiquing its strengths and weaknesses, and anticipating any changes for the next lesson. Ross (1990) defines reflection as "a way of thinking about educational matters that involves the ability to make rational choices and to assume responsibility for those choices" (p. 98). Teachers can reflect before, during, and after a lesson. Before a lesson, teachers should check students' prior knowledge. Reflecting on what is known and how the students learn best will inform teachers about the best instructional practices to choose. In the example above, the experienced teacher, Elaine, built upon the students' understanding of word recognition skills by reminding them, through the think-alouds, how real readers use them to decode unknown words.

During a lesson, teachers often reflect on the spot and take advantage of teachable moments or change the direction of a lesson based on student feedback. During the middle of a minilesson on letter writing, Jennifer discovered that her students did not know the term "greeting." The students struggled with the term when they saw it written next to the "Dear Friend" example on their sample letters.

Jennifer quickly remembered (reflected about) a previous lesson with her third graders and recalled its success. Just before a PTA open house the previous month, Jennifer had her students role-play introducing their parents to her. She had taught them an appropriate greeting upon arriving in their classroom: "Hello, Miss Jennifer, I would like to introduce my parents, Mr. and Mrs. Thompson. This is my teacher, Miss Jennifer." By reflecting on the success of the role-playing and the open house introductions, Jennifer was able to make a connection to the new lesson. She discussed the greeting they had learned and its similarity to a greeting in a friendly letter—saying hello to the reader of the letter. As a result, the term "greeting" took on a new meaning for them. Reflection during the lesson helped Miss Jennifer connect to a prior lesson and assist students in learning the unknown word.

Reflection after the lesson is more commonly thought of as necessary to good teaching. Looking back and deciding how effective the lesson was for the students and teacher in meeting the predetermined goals of instruction is a sign of a teacher acting professionally. In terms of word recognition skills, teachers should check to see if their students are applying the skills when they are reading. For struggling readers, using word recognition skills may be a stop-and-do activity—"Did you go back and try to sound out this new word?" More experienced readers may apply word recognition skills unconsciously as they read—"I noticed when you were reading that you stopped after that sentence with the new vocabulary word and went back to reread it." Thinking back over these two examples of observing two oral readers, the teacher may have reflected that her students understood a variety of word recognition skills during oral reading events. She had reason to feel confident that her time spent working with these skills was well worth it.

Conclusion

So how do teachers create independent readers? By equipping their students with word recognition skills while immersing them in all types of reading and writing. No matter what reading philosophy a teacher espouses, or whether teaching in the primary, intermediate, middle school, secondary, or ESL classroom, teaching word recognition skills is an important, necessary element to help students become better readers. We hope this book provides teachers with resources they can use to support their classroom reading instruction and understand the connection between word recognition skills and comprehension, as they go about the important task of helping their students become lifelong independent readers.

APPENDICES

APPENDIX A

GENERALIZATION	NO. OF WORDS CONFORMING	NO. OF EXCEPTIONS	% OF UTILITY
1. When there are two vowels side by side, the long sound of the first one is heard and the second is usually silent.	309 (bead) †	377 (chief) †	45
2. When a vowel is in the middle of a one-syllable word, the vowel is short.	408	249	62
As middle letter	191 (dress)	84 (scold)	69
One of the middle two letters in a word of four letters	191 (rest)	135 (told)	59
One vowel *within* a word of more than four letters	26 (splash)	30 (fight)	46
3. If the only vowel letter is at the end of a word, the letter usually stands for a long sound.	23 (he)	8 (to)	74
4. When there are two vowels, one of which is final *e*, the first vowel is long and the *e* is silent.	180 (bone)	108 (done)	63
*5. The *r* gives the preceding vowel a sound that is neither long nor short.	484 (horn)	134 (wire)	78
6. The first vowel is usually long and the second silent in the digraphs *ai, ea, oa,* and *ui.*	179	92	66
ai	43 (nail)	24 (said)	64
ea	101 (bead)	51 (head)	66
oa	34 (boat)	1 (cupboard)	97
ui	1 (suit)	16 (build)	6
7. In the phonogram *ie,* the *i* is silent and the *e* has a long sound.	8 (field)	39 (friend)	17

(continued)

---

† Words in parentheses are examples—either of words that conform or of exceptions, depending on the column.

* Generalizations marked with an asterisk were found "useful" according to the criteria.

Source: The Utility of Phonic Generalizations in the Primary Grades, by Theodore Clymer (1996), *Reading Teacher, 50*(3), 182–187. Reprinted by permission of the International Reading Association.

GENERALIZATION	NO. OF WORDS CONFORMING	NO. OF EXCEPTIONS	% OF UTILITY
*8. Words having double *e* usually have the long *e* sound.	85 (seem)	2 (been)	98
9. When words end with silent *e*, the preceding *a* or *i* is long.	164 (cake)	108 (have)	60
*10. In *ay* the *y* is silent and gives *a* its long sound.	36 (play)	10 (always)	78
11. When the letter *i* is followed by the letters *gh*, the *i* usually stands for its long sound and the *gh* is silent.	22 (high)	9 (neighbor)	71
12. When *a* follows *w* in a word, it usually has the sound *a* as in *was*.	15 (watch)	32 (swan)	32
13. When *e* is followed by *w*, the vowel sound is the same as represented by *oo*.	9 (blew)	17 (sew)	35
14. The two letters *ow* make the long *o* sound.	50 (own)	35 (down)	59
15. *W* is sometimes a vowel and follows the vowel digraph rule.	50 (crow)	75 (threw)	40
*16. When *y* is the final letter in a word, it usually has a vowel sound.	169 (dry)	32 (tray)	84
17. When *y* is used as a vowel in words, it sometimes has the sound of long *i*.	29 (fly)	170 (funny)	15
18. The letter *a* has the same sound (ô) when followed by *l*, *w*, and *u*.	61 (all)	65 (canal)	48
19. When *a* is followed by *r* and final *e*, we expect to hear the sound heard in *care*.	9 (dare)	1 (are)	90
*20. When *c* and *h* are next to each other, they make only one sound.	103 (peach)	0	100
*21. *Ch* is usually pronounced as it is in *kitchen*, *catch*, and *chair*, not like *sh*.	99 (catch)	5 (machine)	95
*22. When *c* is followed by *e* or *i*, the sound of *s* is likely to be heard.	66 (cent)	3 (ocean)	96
*23. When the letter *c* is followed by *o* or *a* the sound of *k* is likely to be heard.	143 (camp)	0	100
24. The letter *g* often has a sound similar to that of *j* in *jump* when it precedes the letter *i* or *e*.	49 (engine)	28 (give)	64
*25. When *ght* is seen in a word, *gh* is silent.	30 (fight)	0	100
26. When a word begins *kn*, the *k* is silent.	10 (knife)	0	100
27. When a word begins with *wr*, the *w* is silent.	8 (write)	0	100
*28. When two of the same consonants are side by side, only one is heard.	334 (carry)	3 (suggest)	99

(continued)

GENERALIZATION	NO. OF WORDS CONFORMING	NO. OF EXCEPTIONS	% OF UTILITY
*29. When a word ends in *ck*, it has the same last sound as in *look*.	46 (brick)	0	100
*30. In most two-syllable words, the first syllable is accented.	828 (famous)	143 (polite)	85
*31. If *a, in, re, ex, de,* or *be* is the first syllable in a word, it is usually unaccented.	86 (belong)	13 (insect)	87
*32. In most two-syllable words that end in a consonant followed by *y*, the syllable is accented and the last is unaccented.	101 (baby)	4 (supply)	96
33. One vowel letter in an accented syllable has its short sound.	547 (city)	356 (lady)	61
34. When *y* or *ey* is seen in the last syllable that is not accented, the long sound of *e* is heard.	0	157 (baby)	0
35. When *ture* is the final syllable in a word, it is unaccented.	4 (picture)	0	100
36. When *tion* is the final syllable in a word, it is unaccented.	5 (station)	0	100
37. In many two- and three-syllable words, the final *e* lengthens the vowel in the last syllable.	52 (invite)	62 (gasoline)	46
38. If the first vowel sound in a word is followed by two consonants, the first syllable usually ends with the first of the two consonants.	404 (bullet)	159 (singer)	72
39. If the first vowel sound in a word is followed by a single consonant, that consonant usually begins the second syllable.	190 (over)	237 (oven)	44
*40. If the last syllable of a word ends in *le*, the consonant preceding the *le* usually begins the last syllable.	62 (tumble)	2 (buckle)	97
*41. When the first vowel element in a word is followed by *th, ch,* or *sh*, these symbols are not broken when the word is divided into syllables and may go with either the first or second syllable.	30 (dishes)	0	100
42. In a word of more than one syllable, the letter *v* usually goes with the preceding vowel to form a syllable.	53 (cover)	20 (clover)	73
43. When a word has only one vowel letter, the vowel sound is likely to be short.	433 (hid)	322 (kind)	57
*44. When there is one *e* in a word that ends in a consonant, the *e* usually has a short sound.	85 (leg)	27 (blew)	76
*45. When the last syllable is the sound *r*, it is unaccented.	188 (butter)	9 (appear)	95

APPENDIX B

ROOT	MEANING	EXAMPLES
anthrop	man	anthropology, anthropomorphic
aqua	water	aquatic, aquamarine, aquarium
astr	star	asteroid, astronaut, astronomy,
aud	hear	audio, auditorium, auditory
bio	life, living things	biography, biology
cap	head	capital, capitol, captain
circ	ring	circle, circus, circular
civ	citizen	civics, civil, civilian,
color	color	colorful, colorless, discolor
cycl	ring, circle	bicycle, cycle, cyclone
demo	the people	democratic, demonstration, demagogue
dent	tooth	dental, dentist, indent
dict	say	dictate, dictum, predict
div	separate	divide, division, divisive
duc	lead	abduct, conduct, educate
equ	equal, fair	equal, equality, equator
fort	strong	fort, fortitude, fortify
geo	earth	geography, geology, geometry
graph	something written	autograph, telegraph, graphic
gram	letter	diagram, monogram, telegram
ject	hurl or throw	eject, project, reject
form	shape	reform, transform, uniform
logo	science or study	logical, sociology, zoology

mari	sea	marine, mariner, submarine
meter	measure	centimeter, diameter, thermometer
min	small	minor, miniature, minute
mob	move	automobile, mobile, mobility
mort	death	immortal, mortal, mortician
mov	move	movable, movement, remove
multi	many	multilevel, multiple, multicolored
omni	all	omniscient, omnipresent, omnivorous
onym	name	anonymous, homonym, synonym
phon	sound	phonetics, phonics, phonograph
poly	many	monopoly, polygon, polysyllable
port	carry	portable, portage, transport
prim	first	preprimer, primary, primer
psych	mind	psychology, psychiatrist, psychoanalysis
trans	across, over	transatlantic, transfer, transform
vaca	empty	vacancy, vacant, vacation
vict	conquer	convict, victim, victory
vis	see	television, visible, vision
vit	life	vita, vital, vitality

APPENDIX C

PREFIX	MEANING	EXAMPLES
ab	away from	absent
ad	to, toward	advance
ante	before	anteroom
anti	against	antipathy
bi	having two	bilingual
com	with, next to	combine
con	with, next to	concert
dis	away, apart	disengage
em	in	empower
en	in	enlist
fore	before, front	foreman
il	not	illegal
im	not	impartial
in	not	inactive
inter	between, among	interfere
intro	into, within	introduction
ir	not	irregular
mid	middle	predetermine
pro	before, moving forward	prohibit
re	back, again	react
semi	half, partly	semicircle
sub	under, beneath, below	subconscious
super	over, above, on top of	superimpose
trans	across, over	transport
tri	having three	tricycle
ultra	beyond, excessive	ultramodern
un	not	unfair
under	too little, not enough	undernourished

APPENDIX D

SUFFIX	MEANING	EXAMPLES
able	able to	likable
al	like or suitable for	annual
ant	hat has, does, or shows	accountant
ary	relating to, connected with	dictionary
ento	become or cause to be	strengthen
ence	act, fact, result	excellence
er	one who	teacher
ette	little	statuette
ful	full of, quality of having	helpful
fy	to make, cause, become	intensify
ial	like or suitable for	perennial
ible	able to	legible
ic	of, having to do with	volcanic
ile	of, having to do with	docile
ing	the act or instance of	walking
ion	the act or condition of	correction
ious	having, characterized by	anxious
ish	of, like	boyish
ism	the act, practice, result of	patriotism
ist	a person who	publicist
ity	state, character, condition	possibility
ive	of, relating to, belonging to	creative
less	without, lacking	penniless
ment	a result, product	improvement
ness	state, quality, or instance of being	togetherness
ous	having, full of	dangerous
s	plural	girls
tion	the act of, the state of	correction
ty	quality of, condition of	novelty
y	having, full of	sticky

APPENDIX E

FIRST HUNDRED

First 25 Group 1a	Second 25 Group 1b	Third 25 Group 1c	Fourth 25 Group 1d
the	or	will	number
of	one	up	no
and	had	other	way
a	by	about	could
to	word	out	people
in	but	many	my
is	not	then	than
you	what	them	first
that	all	these	water
it	were	so	been
he	we	some	call
was	when	her	who
for	your	would	oil
on	can	make	now
are	said	like	find
as	there	him	long
with	use	into	down
his	an	time	day
they	each	has	did
I	which	look	get
at	she	two	come
be	do	more	made
this	how	write	may
have	their	go	part
from	if	see	over

Common suffixes: s, ing, ed

The New Instant Word List, by Edward Fry (1980), in *Reading Teacher, 34*(3), 284–289. Reprinted by permission of the International Reading Association.

SECOND HUNDRED

First 25 Group 2a	Second 25 Group 2b	Third 25 Group 2c	Fourth 25 Group 2d
new	great	put	kind
sound	where	end	hand
take	help	does	picture
only	through	another	again
little	much	well	change
work	before	large	off
know	line	must	play
place	right	big	spell
year	too	even	air
live	mean	such	away
me	old	because	animal
back	any	turn	house
give	same	here	point
most	tell	why	page
very	boy	ask	letter
after	follow	went	mother
thing	come	men	answer
our	want	read	found
just	show	need	study
name	also	land	still
good	around	different	learn
sentence	form	home	should
man	three	us	American
think	small	move	world
say	set	try	high

Common suffixes: s, ing, ed, er, ly, est

THIRD HUNDRED

First 25 Group 3a	Second 25 Group 3b	Third 25 Group 3c	Fourth 25 Group 3d
every	left	until	idea
near	don't	children	enough
add	few	side	eat
food	while	feet	face
between	along	car	watch
own	might	mile	far
below	close	night	Indian
country	something	walk	real
plant	seem	white	almost
last	next	sea	let
school	hard	began	above
father	open	grow	girl
keep	example	took	sometimes
tree	begin	river	mountain
never	life	four	cut
start	always	carry	young
city	those	state	talk
earth	both	once	soon
eye	paper	book	list
light	together	hear	song
thought	got	stop	leave
head	group	without	family
under	often	second	body
story	run	late	music
saw	important	miss	color

Common suffixes: s, ing, ed, er, ly, est

APPENDIX F

AN INTRODUCTION TO ENGLISH ORTHOGRAPHY

CONSONANTS

b	ball
d	dust
f	fast
h	hat
j	jar
k	kite
l	last
m	man
n	near
p	put
qu	quack
r	ran
t	tack
v	vase
w	wall
x	x-ray
z	zoo

VARIANT CONSONANTS

c, g — cot, cent, get, giraffe

DIGRAPHS WITH h

ch	chin / school / charade
gh	ghost
ph	phone
sh	shine
th	thin / then
wh	whale / whom

DIGRAPHS WITH FIRST SILENT LETTER

ck	neck
gn	gnat
kn	know
wr	wren

DIGRAPH CLUSTER FOLLOWING A SHORT VOWEL

dge	ledge
tch	match

ADDITIONAL DIGRAPH

ng — song

BLENDS—INITIAL

r	green
l	clear
s	spine / strap
tw	twine

BLENDS—FINAL

ld	held
lk	talk
nd	pond
nk	sink
nt	want

SPECIAL COMBINATION OF CONSONANT AND VOWEL

ci	crucial
si	pension
ti	nation

VOWELS

SINGLE—SHORT

a	ă	apple
e	ĕ	elephant
i	ĭ	itch
o	ŏ	octopus
u	ŭ	umbrella

SINGLE—LONG

a	ā	ape
e	ē	event
i	ī	ivy
o	ō	open
u and ū		uniform
oo		crude

SINGLE—THIRD SOUND

a	ä	father (fäther)
o	oo	move (mŏve)
u	oŏ	bush (boŏsh)

SCHWA ə IN UNACCENTED SYLLABLES

a	əmong
e	blankət
i	Aprəl
o	bacən

DIGRAPHS/DIPHTHONGS WITH a

ai as /ā/	pain
ay as /ā/	play
au as /aw/	caution
aw as /aw/	straw

DIGRAPHS WITH e

ee as	/ē/	weed
ea as	/ē/	meat
	/ĕ/	dead
	/ā/	great
ie as	/ē/	belief
	/ī/	tie
ei as	/ē/ (after c)	receive
		rein
	/ā/	
ey as	/ē/	monkey
	/ā/	prey

DIGRAPHS AND DIPHTHONGS WITH o

oa as	/ō/	bloat
oi as	/oy/	noise
oy as	/oy/	toy
oo as	/oo/	soon
	/ŏŏ/	took
ou as	/ow/	trout
	/ŭ/	young
	/ŏ/	soul
	/oo/	troupe
ow as	/ow/	owl
	/ō/	blow

From *Striking a Balance: Positive Practices for Early Literacy,* by Nancy Lee Cecil. Copyright © 1999 by Holcomb Hathaway, Publishers (Scottsdale, AZ).

APPENDIX G

Websites

Learning to read: Resources for language arts and reading research
www.toread.com

Beginning reading instruction
www.just4kids.org/html/bri.html

International Reading Association
www.ira.org

National Council of Teachers of English
www.ncte.org

Reading Recovery Council of North America
www.readingrecovery.org

Word Play
www.wolinshkyweb.com/word.htm

Reading Rainbow
gpn.unl.edu/rainbow

Teachers.Net Reading
www.teachers.net

Games for Learning
www.games2learn.com

Mrs. Alphabet Newsletter
www.shagmail.com/sub-alpha.html

Software

A to Zap! (Wings for Learning, Inc.)
A+ Reading Island Journey (Sunburst)
Ace Detective; Ace Inquiry; Ace Report (Mind Play)
ASL Fingerspelling (Scott Baertner)

Arthur (Living Books)

Bailey's Book House (Edmark Corporation)

Bubble Land Dictionary Vol. 1 & 2 (Ednovation)

Build Vocabulary Skills CD (Queue, Inc.)

Carmen Sandiego Word Detective (grades 3–7) (Mattel Interactive)

Curious George Learns Phonics (Houghton Mifflin)

Early English for Kids (Red Horse Productions)

ESL Renegdes (Gamco Education Material)

Great Beginning (Teacher Support Software, Inc.)

Kid Phonics (Knowledge Adventure, Inc.)

KidPix Studio Deluxe (Broderbund)

KidsTime (Great Wave Software)

Learn Letters; Learn Sounds; Bridges to Reading (Owl & Mouse Educational Software)

Memory Building Blocks (Sunburst Communications)

Oregon Trail (MECC)

Phonics Alive and Phonics Alive (Knowledge Adventure, Inc.)

Reader Rabbit (The Learning Company)

Reading Blaster (Davidson)

Reading Mansion Software (Games2Learn)

School House Rock! Grammar Rock (Creative Wonders)

SchoolHouse Series (Creative Wonders)

Stickybear's Reading Comprehension (Optimum Resources, Inc.)

StoryBook Weaver Delux (MECC)

Thinking Things (Edmark)

30 Froggy Phonics (Ingenuity Works, Inc.)

Word Munchers (MECC)

Writing Center (The Learning Company)

STUCO-SLIDE GRID

(discussed on p. 79 of text)

16"

21"

1. Create the grid above on a piece of poster board.
2. Cut rectangles of white paper 3" × 2.5". "Students write, draw, diagram, design, type, or interpret in visual form what they want on their slides" (p. 364).
3. Rubber-cement the paper slips to the grid.
4. Take the grid to an offset printer to make an 8.5" × 11" negative.
5. Cut the negative into individual slides along the clear lines.
6. Color in the clear areas on the negatives using markers.
7. Place the negative into a slide sleeve.
8. Arrange the slide show.

Source: Wilson, C. (1996). Stuco-slides enhance literacy and content learning. *Reading Teacher, 50*(4), 364–365.

REFERENCES

Adams, M. J. (1990). *Beginning to read: Thinking and learning about print.* Cambridge, MA: MIT Press.

Anderson, R. C., Hiebert, E. H., Scott, J. A., & Wilkinson, I. A. G. (1985). *Becoming a nation of readers: The report of the commission on reading.* Washington, DC: National Institute of Education.

Armstrong, T. (1994). *Multiple intelligences in the classroom.* Alexandria, VA: Association for School Curriculum and Development.

Atwell, N. (1987). *In the middle.* Portsmouth, NH: Boynton/Cook.

Baumann, J. F., Hoffman, J. V., Moon, J., & Duffy-Hester A.M. (1998). Where are teachers' voices in the phonics/whole language debate? Results from a survey of U.S. elementary teachers. *The Reading Teacher, 51*(8), 636–650.

Bryan, J. (1998). K-W-W-L: Questioning the known. *The Reading Teacher, 51*(7), 618–620.

Bullough, R., & Gitlin, A. (1991). Toward educative communities: Teacher education and the development of the reflective practitioner. In B. R. Tabachnick & K. Zeichner (Eds.), Issues and practices in inquiry-oriented teacher education (pp. 35–55). London: Falmer Press.

Burns, P. C., Roe, B. D., & Ross, E. P. (1996). *Teaching reading in today's elementary schools.* Boston: Houghton Mifflin.

Calkins, L. M. (1986). *The art of teaching writing.* Portsmouth, NH: Heinemann.

Camp, D. (2000). It takes two: Teaching with twin texts of fact and fiction. *The Reading Teacher, 53*(5), 400–408.

Cecil, N. L. (2001). *Activities for striking a balance in early literacy.* Scottsdale, AZ: Holcomb Hathaway, Publishers.

Chall, J. S. (1983). *Vocabularies for reading: How large? What kind?* (ERIC Document Reproduction Service No. ED 235 460).

Chard, D. J. (1995). *Understanding the primary role of word recognition in the reading process: Synthesis of research on beginning reading,* Technical Report No. 15. (ERIC Document Reproduction Service No. ED 386 862).

Choate, J. S., Enright, B. E., Miller, L. J., Poteet, J. A., & Rakes, T. A. (1995). *Curriculum-based assessment and programming* (3d ed.). Boston: Allyn and Bacon.

Clay, M. M. (1991). *Becoming literate: The construction of inner control.* Portsmouth, NH: Heinemann.

Clay, M. M. (1993). *An observation survey of early literacy achievement.* Portsmouth, NH: Heinemann.

Clymer, T. (1996). The utility of phonic generalizations in the primary grades. *The Reading Teacher, 50*(3), 182–187.

Cramer, G., Hurst, B., & Wilson, C. (1996). *Teacher study groups for professional development.* Phi Delta Kappan Fastback. Bloomington, IN: Phi Delta Kappa Educational Foundation.

Cunningham, P. M., & Hall, D. P. (1999). *The teacher's guide to the four blocks: A multi-method, multilevel framework for grades 1–3.* Greensboro, NC: Carson-Dellosa Publishing.

Cunningham, P. M., Hall, D. P., & Heggie, T. (1994). *Making words: Multilevel, hands-on developmentally appropriate spelling and phonics activities.* Torrance, CA: Good Apple.

Davey, B. (1983). Think-aloud—Modeling the cognitive processes of reading comprehension. *Journal of Reading, 27,* 44–47.

Flynt, E. S., & Cooter, R. B. (2000). *Reading inventory for the classroom,* 4th ed. Upper Saddle River, NJ: Merrill.

Fountas, I. C., & Pinnell, G. S. (1996). *Guided reading: Good first teaching for all children.* Portsmouth, NH: Heinemann.

Fry, E. (1977). *Elementary reading instruction.* New York: McGraw-Hill.

Fry, E. (1980). The new instant word list. *The Reading Teacher, 34*(3), 284–289.

Gambrell, L. B. (1996). Creating classroom cultures that foster reading motivation. *The Reading Teacher, 50*(1), 14–23.

Gardner, H. (1983). *Frames of the mind: The theory of multiple intelligences* (10th ed.). New York: BasicBooks.

Gentry, J. R. (1997). *My kid can't spell! Understanding and assisting your child's literacy development.* Portsmouth, NH: Heinemann.

Glazier, T. F. (1993). *The least you should know about vocabulary building word roots.* New York: Harcourt Brace Jovanovich.

Goodman, K. (1986). *What's whole in whole language?* Portsmouth, NH: Heinemann.

Graves, D. H. (1991). *Build a literate classroom.* Portsmouth, NH: Heinemann.

Griffith, P. L., & Olson, M. W. (1992). Phonemic awareness helps beginning readers break the code. *The Reading Teacher, 45*(7), 516–533.

Haggard, M. R. (1986). The vocabulary self-collection strategy: Using student interest and world knowledge to enhance vocabulary growth. *Journal of Reading, 29*(7), 634–642.

Harris, T. L., & Hodges, R. E. (1995) *The literacy dictionary: The vocabulary of reading and writing.* Newark, DE: International Reading Association.

Harris, A. J., & Sipay, E. R. (1990). *How to increase reading ability: A guide to developmental & remedial methods* (9th ed.). New York: Longman.

Harste, J. C. (1989). *New policy guidelines for reading: Connecting research and practice.* Urbana, IL: National Council of Teachers of English.

Harste, J. C., Short, C., & Burke, C. (1998). *Creating classrooms for authors.* Portsmouth, NH: Heinemann.

Holmes, J. A. (1965). Basic assumptions underlying the substrata-factor theory. *Reading Research Quarterly, 1,* 5–27.

Hurst, B. (2000). How do you get students to read in content area classrooms? *The Transescent, 24*(4), 24–25.

International Reading Association. (1997a). *Phonemic awareness and the teaching of reading* [A Position Statement]. Newark, DE: IRA Board of Directors.

International Reading Association. (1997b). *The role of phonics in reading instruction* [A Position Statement]. Newark, DE: IRA Board of Directors.

Johns, J. L. (1986). *Handbook for remediation of reading difficulties.* Englewood Cliffs, NJ: Prentice Hall.

Karlin, R. (1981). *Teaching reading in high school: Improving reading in the content areas* (4th ed.). New York: Harper & Row.

Lapp, D., Flood, J., Ranck-Buhr, W., Van Dyke, J., & Spacek, S. (1997). "Do you really just want us to talk about this book?": A closer look at book clubs as an instructional tool. In Paratore, J. R., & McCormack, R. L. (Eds.), *Peer talk in the classroom: Learning from research* (pp. 6–23). Newark, DE: International Reading Association.

McCourt-Lewis, A. A. (1980). *Vocabulary development synonym for sense-ible word identification instruction.* (ERIC Document Reproduction Service No. ED 190 81).

Manzo, A. V. (1969). The ReQuest procedure. *Journal of Reading, 11,* 123–126.

Manzo, A. V. (1975). Guided reading procedure. *Journal of Reading 18,* 287–291.

National Institutes of Health. (2000). *National reading panel reports combination of teaching phonics, word sounds, giving feedback on oral reading most effective way to teach reading.* Washington, DC: National Institutes of Health.

Ogle, D. (1986). K-W-L: A teaching model that develops active reading in expository text. *The Reading Teacher, 39*(6), 564–570.

Pikulski, J. J. (1997–98). So much to do, so little time. *Reading Today, 15*(3), 36.

Pinnell, G. S., & Fountas, I. C. (1998). *Word matters.* Portsmouth, NH: Heinemann Educational Books.

Piper, T. (1998). *Language and learning: The home and school years* (2d ed.). Upper Saddle River, NJ: Prentice Hall.

Richgels, D. J., Poremba, K. J., & McGee, L. M. (1996). Kindergartners talk about print: Phonemic awareness in meaningful contexts. *The Reading Teacher, 49*(8), 632–642.

Robinson, F. (1961). *Effective study.* New York: Harper & Row.

Robinson, R. D., McKenna, M. C., & Wedman, J. M. (1996). *Issues and trends in literacy education.* Boston: Allyn & Bacon.

Ross, D. D. (1990). Programmatic structures for the preparation of reflective teachers. In R. T. Clift, W. R. Houston, & M. C. Puguach (Eds.), *Encouraging reflective practice in education: An analysis of issues and programs* (pp. 97–118). New York: Teachers College Press.

Routman, R. (1991). *Invitations: Changing as teachers and learners.* Portsmouth, NH: Heinemann.

Routman, R. (1996). *Literacy at the crossroads.* Portsmouth, NH: Heinemann.

Routman, R. (2000). *Conversations.* Portsmouth, NH: Heinemann.

Routman, R., & Butler A. (1996). How do I actually *teach* reading now that I am using literature? *School Talk, 1*(3). Urbana, IL: National Council of Teachers of English.

Samuels, S. J. (1988). Decoding and automaticity: Helping poor readers become automatic at word recognition. *The Reading Teacher, 41*(8), 756–760.

Scott, J. A. & Ehri, L. C. (1990). Sight word reading in prereaders: Use of logographic vs. alphabetic access routes. *Journal of Reading Behavior, 22*(2), 149–66.

Searfoss, L. W. (1975). Radio reading. *The Reading Teacher 29,* 295–296.

Short, K. G., Giorgis, C., & Pritchard, T. G. (April, 1993). *Principal study groups and teacher study groups: An interactive and innovative approach to curriculum change.* Paper presented at American Educational Research Association, 1993 Annual Meeting, Atlanta.

Smith, F. (1975). *Comprehension and learning: A conceptual framework for teachers.* New York: Holt, Rinehart & Winston.

Smith, F. (1998a). *The book of learning and forgetting.* New York: Teachers College Press.

Smith, F. (1988b). *Understanding reading* (4th ed.). Hillsdale, NJ: Lawrence Erlbaum Associates.

Snow, C. E., Burns, M. S., & Griffin, P. (1998). *Preventing reading difficulties in young children.* Washington, DC: National Academy Press.

Spargo, E., Ed. (1974). *Topics for the restless.* Providence, RI: Jamestown Publishers.

Stahl, S. (2000). *Fluency oriented reading instruction.* Summer institute of the Center for the Improvement of Early Reading Achievement, Athens, GA.

Stauffer, R. G. (1969). *Directing reading maturity as a cognitive process.* New York: Harper & Row.

Stevens, K. C. (1982). Can we improve reading by teaching background information? *Journal of Reading, 25,* 326–329.

Stotsky, S. (1983). Research on reading/writing relationships: A synthesis and suggested direction. *Language Arts, 60,* 627–642.

Strickland, D. S., & Morrow, L. M. (1989). *Emerging literacy: Young children learn to read and write.* Newark, DE: International Reading Association.

Taylor, W. (1953). Cloze procedure: A new tool for measuring readability. *Journalism Quarterly, 30,* 415–433.

Tonjes, M. J., & Zintz, M. V. (1981). *Teaching reading/thinking/study skills in content classrooms.* Dubuque, IA: Wm. C. Brown Co.

Vacca, R. T., & Vacca, J. L. (1999). *Content area reading: Literacy and learning across the curriculum* (6th ed.). New York: Addison-Wesley.

Veatch, J. (1966). *Reading in the elementary school.* New York: Ronald Press.

Vygotsky, L. S. (1978). *Thought and language.* Cambridge, MA: MIT Press.

Wilde, S. (1997). *What's a schwa sound anyway?* Portsmouth, NH: Heinemann.

Wilson, C. (1996). Stuco-slides enhance literacy and content learning. *The Reading Teacher, 50*(4), 364–365.

Wishon, P. M., Crabtree, K., & Jones, M. E. (1998). *Curriculum for the primary years: An integrative approach.* Upper Saddle River, NJ: Merrill/Prentice Hall.

Yopp, H. K. (1992). Developing phonemic awareness in young children. *The Reading Teacher, 45*(9), 696–703.

Zakaluk, B. L., & Sealey, D. B. (1988). Teaching reading to Cree-speaking children: Instructional implications from an interactive model of reading. *Reading Canada Lecture, 6*(20), 93–99.

Additional
READINGS

Akamatsu, N. (1999). The effects of first language orthographic features on word recognition processing in English as a Second Language. *Reading and Writing: An Interdisciplinary Journal, 11*(4), 381–403.

Allen, L. (1998). An integrated strategies approach: Making word identification instruction work for beginning readers. *The Reading Teacher, 52*(3), 254–268.

Armbruster, B. B., & Nagy, W. E. (1992). Vocabulary in content area lessons. *The Reading Teacher, 45*(7), 550–551.

Armster, J. (1987). Test review: Receptive one-word picture vocabulary test. *The Reading Teacher, 40*(4), 452–455.

Barrentine, S. J. (1996). Engaging with reading through interactive read-alouds. *The Reading Teacher, 50*(3), 36–43.

Bear, D. R., Invernizzi, M., Templeton, S., & Johnston, F. (1996). *Words their way: Word study for phonics, vocabulary, and spelling instruction.* Upper Saddle River, NJ: Merrill.

Beaver, J. (1997). *Developmental reading assessment.* Parisippany, NJ: Celebration Press.

Betts, E. A. (1946). *Foundations of reading instruction.* New York: American Book Company.

Blachman, B. A., Tangel, D. M., Ball, E. W., Black, R., & McGraw, C. K. (1999). Developing phonological awareness and word recognition skills: A two-year intervention with low-income, inner-city children. *Reading and Writing: An Interdisciplinary Journal, 11*(3), 239–273.

Bolton, F., and Snowball, D. (1993). *Teaching Spelling: A practical resource.* Portsmouth, NH: Heinemann.

Bryant, D. P., Ugel, N., Thompson, S., & Hamff, A. (1999). Instructional strategies for content-area reading instruction. *Intervention in School and Clinic, 34*(5), 293–302.

Burgstahler, S, & Utterback, L. (2000). *New kids on the net: Internet activities in elementary language arts.* Boston, MA: Allyn and Bacon.

Busink, R. (1997). Reading and phonological awareness: What we have learned and how we can use it. *Reading Research and Instruction, 36*(3), 199–215.

Chard, D. J., & Osborn, J. (1999). Word recognition instruction: Paving the road to successful reading. *Intervention in School and Clinic, 34*(5), 271–277.

Cunningham, P. M. (1979). A compare/contrast theory of mediated word identification. *The Reading Teacher, 32*(7), 774–778.

Cunningham, P. M. (1988). When all else fails . . . *The Reading Teacher, 41*(8), 800–805.

Cunningham, P. M. (1990). The names test: A quick assessment of decoding ability. *The Reading Teacher, 44*(2), 124–129.

Cunningham, P. M. (1995). *Phonics they use: Words in reading and writing* (2d ed.). New York: HarperCollins.

Cunningham, P. M. (1998). *Classrooms that work: They can all read and write.* Addison-Wesley.

Cunningham, J. W., Cunningham, P. M., Hoffman, J. V., & Yopp. H. R. (1998). *Phonemic awareness and the teaching of reading: A position statement from the board of directors of the International Reading Association.* Newark, DE: International Reading Association.

Cunningham, P. M., & Hall, D. P. (1994). *Making big words: Multilevel, hands-on spelling and phonics activities.* Torrance, CA: Good Apple.

Cunningham, P. M., & Hall, D. P. (2000). *Making more words: Multilevel, hands-on phonics and spelling activities.* Torrance, CA: Good Apple.

DeSerres, B. (1990). Putting vocabulary in context. *The Reading Teacher, 43*(8), 612–613.

Eeds, M. (1985). Bookwords: Using a beginning word list of high frequency words from children's literature K–3. *The Reading Teacher, 38*(4), 418–423.

Eeds, M., & Cockrum, W. A. (1985). Teaching word meanings by expanding schemata vs. dictionary work vs. reading in context. *The Journal of Reading, 28*(6), 492–497.

Eeds, M., & Wells, D. (1989). Grand conversations: An exploration of meaning construction in literature study groups. *Research in the Teaching of English, 23*(1), 4–29.

Farr, R. (1991). *Reading: What can be measured?* (2d ed.) Newark, DE: International Reading Association.

Fielding, L. G. (1998–1999). Making balanced use of cues when reading. *The Reading Teacher, 52*(4), 392–393.

Gaskins, I. W., Ehri, L. C., Cress, C., O'Hara, C., & Donnelly, K. (1997). Procedures for word learning: Making discoveries about words. *The Reading Teacher, 50*(4), 312–327.

Gentry, J. R. (1993). *Teaching kids to spell.* Portsmouth, NH: Heinemann.

Goodall, M. (1984). Can four year olds "read" words in the environment? *The Reading Teacher, 37*(6), 478–482.

Groff, P. (1981). Teaching reading by syllables. *The Reading Teacher, 34*(6), 659–663.

Gunning, T. G. (1995). Word building: A strategic approach to the teaching of phonics. *The Reading Teacher, 48*(6), 484–489.

Gutierrez, C., Vera, F., & DeCurtis, L. (1999). Word definition skills in Spanish-speaking children with language impairment. *Communication Disorders Quarterly, 21*(1), 23–31.

Hare, V. C. (1984). What's in a word? A review of young children's difficulties with the construct "word." *The Reading Teacher, 37*(4), 360–364.

Harste, J., Short, K. G., with Burke, C. (1998). *Creating classrooms for authors.* Portsmouth, NH: Heinemann.

Harvey, S., & Goudvis, A. (2000). *Strategies that work: Teaching comprehension to enhance understanding.* York, ME: Stenhouse Publishers.

Herman, P. A. (1985). The effect of repeated readings on reading rate, speech, and word recognition. *Reading Research Quarterly, 20*(5), 553–565.

Hindley, J. (1996). *In the company of children.* York, ME: Stenhouse Publishers.

Hirsh-Pasek, K. (1986). Beyond the great debate: Fingerspelling as an alternative route to word identification for deaf or dyslexic readers. *The Reading Teacher, 40*(3), 340–343.

Hurst, B., & Reding, G. (1999). *Keeping the light in your eyes: A guide to helping teachers discover, remember, relive, and rediscover the joy of teaching.* Scottsdale, AZ: Holcomb Hathaway.

Johns, J. L. (1985). *Basic reading inventory* (3d ed.). Dubuque, IA: Kendall-Hunt.

Johns, J. L. (1986). *Handbook for remediation of reading difficulties.* Englewood Cliffs, NJ: Prentice-Hall.

Johnston, F. R. (1998). The reader, the text, and task: Learning words in first grade. *The Reading Teacher, 51*(8), 666–675.

Joseph, L. M. (1998–1999). Word boxes help children with learning disabilities identify and spell words. *The Reading Teacher, 52*(4), 348–356.

Juel, C., & Minden-Cupp, C. (1999–2000). One down and 80,000 to go: Word recognition instruction in the primary grades. *The Reading Teacher, 53*(4), 332–335.

Keene, O., & Zimmerman, S. (1997). *Mosaic of thought: Teaching comprehension in a reader's workshop.* Portsmouth, NH: Heinemann.

Koskinsen, P. S., & Blum, I. H. (1986). Paired repeating reading: A classroom strategy for developing fluent reading. *The Reading Teacher, 40,* 70–75.

Lynch, J. (1998). *Easy lessons for teaching word families: Hands-on lessons that build phonemic awareness, phonics, spelling, reading, and writing skills.* New York: Scholastic Books.

Maclean, R. (1988). Two paradoxes of phonics. *The Reading Teacher, 41*(6), 514–517.

Markham, P. (1999). Captioned videotapes and second-language listening word recognition. *Foreign Language Annals, 32*(3), 321–328.

McKinney, C. (1990). The expert's tic tac toe. *The Reading Teacher, 43*(8), 613.

Nagy, W. (1988). *Teaching vocabulary to improve reading comprehension.* Urbana, IL: National Council of Teachers of English.

Pearson, P. D., Hansen, J., & Gordon, C. (1979). The effect of background knowledge on young children's comprehension of explicit and implicit information. *Journal of Reading Behavior, 11,* 201–209.

Pinnell, G. S., Bird, L. B., & Fountas, I. C. (1999). *Matching books to readers: Using leveled books in guided reading, K–3.* Portsmouth, NH: Heinemann.

Rasinski, T. V., & Padak, N. D. (1996). *Holistic reading strategies: Teaching children who find reading difficult.* Columbus, OH: Merrill.

Richardson, K. (1987). Test review: Decoding skills test (DST). *The Reading Teacher, 41*(2), 220–223.

Smith, F. (1975). *Comprehension and learning.* New York: Holt, Rinehart & Winston.

Smith, F. (1985). *Reading without nonsense* (2d ed.). New York: Teachers College Press.

Snow, C. E., Burns, M. S., & Griffin, P. (1998). *Preventing reading difficulties in young children.* Washington, DC: National Academy Press.

Snow, C. E., Scarborough, H. S., & Burns, M. S. (1999). What speech language pathologists need to know about early reading. *Topics in Language Disorders, 20*(1), 48–58.

Stahl, S. A. (1992). Saying the "p" word: Nine guidelines for exemplary phonic instruction. *The Reading Teacher, 45*(8), 618–625.

Staul, S. A., Duffy-Hester, A. M., & Stahl, K. A. (1998). Everything you wanted to know about phonics (but were afraid to ask). *Reading Research Quarterly, 33*(3), 338–355.

Sutton, C. (1989). Helping the nonnative English speaker with reading. *The Reading Teacher, 42*(9). 684–688.

Swearingen, R., & Allen, D. (2000). *Classroom assessment of reading process* (2d ed.). Boston: Houghton Mifflin.

Trachtenburg, P. (1990). Using children's literature to enhance phonic instruction. *The Reading Teacher, 43*(9), 648–654.

Wagstaff, J. M. (1999). *Teaching reading and writing with word walls: Easy lessons and fresh ideas for creating interactive word walls that build literacy.* New York: Scholastic Books.

Walker, C. M. (1979). High frequency word list for grades 3 through 9. *The Reading Teacher, 32*(7), 803–812.

Walley, C. (1993). An invitation to reading fluency. *The Reading Teacher, 46*(6), 526–527.

White, T. G., Sowell, J., & Yanagihara, A. (1989). *Teaching elementary students to use word-part clues, 42*(4), 302–308.

Willson, V. L., Ruplet, W. H., Rodrigues, M., & Mergen, S. (1999). The relationships among orthographic components of word identification and spelling for grades 1–6. *Reading Research and Instruction, 39*(1), 89–102.

Wuthrick, M. A. (1990). What should I do when they don't know the words: A review of the Literature. *The Reading Teacher, 24*(2), 32–40.

Yopp, H. K. (1995). A test for assessing phonemic awareness in young children. *The Reading Teacher, 49*(1), 20–29.

Yopp, H. K. (1995). Read-aloud books for developing phonemic awareness: An annotated bibliography. *The Reading Teacher, 48*(6), 538–542.

GLOSSARY

affixes The collective name for word parts added either to the beginning of words (prefixes) or the ends of words (suffixes).

alphabet books Books that feature words and pictures using the alphabet. Beginning readers can be asked to make their own alphabet books as a strategy to help them learn to recognize, write, and say letters.

alphabetic principle The understanding that written language in English and other languages is based on print or graphic symbols that stand for spoken sounds and that each letter represents a sound.

anecdotal records Written observations that teachers keep of individual students' targeted social, literacy, or other behavior, usually kept over a planned period of time.

automaticity A term coined by Samuels (1988) that describes a reader's ability to read without having to decode, because the decoding process has become automatic and internalized.

basal reading program An approach to reading instruction that uses a graded collection of student anthologies, teachers' manuals, and additional materials, such as workbooks, transparencies, and software.

big books Large-sized books, usually about 2 feet by 3 feet, from which the teacher reads aloud, enabling small or large groups of children to see the text, which is not possible with regular-sized children's books.

checklist An informal assessment tool in which the teacher or observer places marks next to specified behaviors, skills, or other attributes.

choral reading An oral reading activity in which readers read aloud, in unison or in turn; provides practice in fluency.

chunking The practice of looking at groups of letters together as units to assist in decoding words.

Clay's 5-finger suggestion A set of suggestions in which students are asked to: (1) Look at the picture and think about the story; (2) Reread the sentence and get your mouth ready; (3) Does it sound right? Can I say it that way?; (4) Read on to see if that will help me; (5) Do I see a part that I know in the word?

closed syllable A sound unit that ends with a consonant and usually has a short vowel sound (e.g., the vowel sounds found at the beginning of the words apple, elephant, igloo, octopus, and umbrella).

cloze procedure A means of estimating students' ability to read a given reading passage by deleting every nth (usually fifth, except for primary grades) word to determine whether the text is at the individual student's independent, instructional, or frustrational reading level.

clustering A strategy used to improve fluency or adequate phrasing, in which teachers show readers how to combine two to four words in meaningful groupings and train their eyes to see all the words in a cluster at a glance; especially helpful with English as a Second Language students and other struggling readers.

compound word A word in which two complete words are combined to form a new word.

configuration clues The use that beginning readers make of the outline or general shape of words to help them identify words.

consonant Speech sound made by partially closing the mouth or tongue; all letters other than the vowels of a, e, i, o, and u; or the letters representing speech sounds, such as b, c, d, f.

consonant blend or cluster Two or more consonants that work together with each sound heard, such as /str/ in string, /br/ in brother, /sk/ in skate.

consonant digraphs Two consonants that work together to form one sound, as in /sh/ in ship, /ch/ in chunk, /wh/ in which, and /ph/ in phone.

content-area reading Reading undertaken within a field such as science or math when children are reading informational text.

decoding The process used in reading to interpret the coding system of written language, which allows the reader to translate written words into the appropriate accompanying oral sounds (sounding words out).

diphthong A closely blended or glided vowel sound represented by two letters together, as in /oi/ in oil, or /ou/ in ouch.

directed reading–thinking activity (DR–TA) A comprehension strategy developed by Stauffer (1969), in which the teacher—responding neutrally and accepting all answers—takes the class through a silent reading selection, stopping at various points, and asking students predictional questions.

duet reading An oral reading activity in which the teacher and student read together simultaneously to provide fluency practice.

echo reading An oral reading activity in which the teacher or tutor reads a phrase or two, and the less experienced reader immediately repeats what the teacher or tutor has read while looking at the words.

encoding The process used in writing to record the graphic symbols used to represent oral sound.

fluency The ability to read smoothly and with expression orally or to read silently with understanding and few decoding difficulties.

graphemes The smallest written representation of a sound unit in a word.

grapho-phonemics The study of the relationship between written language (orthography) and spoken language (phonology).

guided reading procedure (GRP) A comprehension instruction strategy developed by Manzo (1975) that can be used to recall details and help organize information; students are asked to read a passage and remember everything they can, then are asked to brainstorm everything they can remember from the passage while the teacher records the details, on the chalkboard or overhead, in the order in which they were mentioned, and then are asked to organize the information individually or in groups in some meaningful way (often using webbing, mapping, or some other kind of visual outlining).

informal assessment Nonstandardized means of gathering information about learners, which tend to be modified as needed and interpreted as considered useful by the teacher or tester.

informal reading inventory (IRI) An individually administered method of assessing approximate reading levels, which the teacher can construct, but it is often a published instrument, under varying developers' or publishers' titles, generally containing graded lists of words, a series of graded passages of increasing difficulty, for the student to read aloud while the teacher marks errors systematically, with retelling and/or comprehension questions following each passage, and a second set to be read silently, that eventually establishes independent, instructional, and frustrational reading levels for each reader.

invented or developmental spelling A temporary process by which young children create their own attempts at writing words, which allows them to use written language as a means of communication earlier than possible otherwise.

K-W-L A strategy developed by Ogle (1986) using a graphic chart with three columns designated K (what we know), W (what we want to learn), and L (what we learned).

language experience approach (LEA) A method of early reading instruction in which the teacher works with an individual or a class, in which students dictate a story as the teacher prints it exactly as stated; the teacher then points to each word and rereads the story, and the student or students read back the story. This and other stories and word banks serve as materials of instruction for reading, writing, speaking, and listening activities, particularly for needed phonics and word recognition work.

long vowel sounds Vowel sounds that sound like the letters they represent (they say their own names), which generally are found in open syllables (syllables ending with a vowel).

mad-libs A learning activity in which students supply parts of speech responses to unknown stories, with the resulting funny story read aloud.

matching cloze exercise A procedure similar to the cloze activity, except that students receive a randomized list of the deleted words.

maze procedure A variation of the cloze procedure in which three choices are provided as possibilities for each deleted word, with the distracter words.

minilesson A short lesson of about 5 to 10 minutes, in which the teacher calls attention to a skill or strategy, giving guided practice, prior to giving students independent practice, and before finally checking for appropriate usage or comprehension.

modified cloze activity A variation of the cloze procedure in which the teacher selects words to delete, depending on the word recognition, comprehension, or vocabulary skills to be developed.

morpheme The smallest meaningful linguistic unit in a word; free morphemes are words that can stand alone as meaning units and cannot be broken into smaller units of meaning; bound morphemes are word parts that must be attached to free morphemes to have meaning.

multiple intelligences (MI) Gardner's (1983) theory that intelligence is expressed in multiple ways including verbal-linguistic, logical-mathematical, musical, visual-spatial, bodily-kinesthetic, interpersonal, intrapersonal, and naturalist.

onset The beginning of a word such as the /dr/ in drive, dream, or drop, used in looking at sets of words, such as word families, and generally paired with rimes.

open syllable A sound unit that ends with a vowel, which usually has a long vowel sound (it says its own name) as in /ta/ in table (tá•ble).

paired reading An oral reading activity in which students read with partners, alternating reading each paragraph or page.

parallel books An activity in which readers write and illustrate a book that uses some or much of the text or structure of the story or original text.

phoneme Smallest unit of sound in the speech stream.

phonemic awareness The recognition that words are made up of sounds, the knowledge that sounds in words can be manipulated, and the ability to determine if words sound alike or different (including rhymes and alliteration).

phonic analysis The means by which words can be recognized by looking at their sound and letter relationship.

phonics The relationship between sounds and their graphic or print representations; the sound–letter relationship.

phonics charts Lists of words that students identify, often within the context of a story, which have shared phonic characteristics collected on a chart.

prefixes Word parts added to the beginning of a root or word.

radio reading A comprehension instructional strategy, developed by Searfoss (1975), in which the teacher divides the students into groups of three to five, with one portion of a content-rich passage assigned to each student, to prepare to read aloud as a radio announcer, asking one question for each member of their group, while the other group members listen without looking at the passage being read aloud.

recreational reading Reading undertaken for pleasure, with the reader choosing the material to be read and no assignments connected to the reading.

ReQuest A comprehension instructional strategy, developed by Manzo (1975), in which the teacher and student silently read a section of text, with students then questioning the teacher orally about the section, followed by the teacher asking questions of the students, and continuing the exchange of roles for several paragraphs.

retellings An informal assessment method in which the teacher asks the student to recount a story or text immediately after the student has been asked to read it either silently or orally.

rime The ending of words that sound and are spelled the same, such as /at/ in cat, sat, rat, used in looking at sets of words, such as word families, and generally paired with onsets.

root The main part of a word, which usually carries the meaning portion of the word and cannot be subdivided further without losing meaning.

rule of thumb A means developed by Veatch (1966) to determine whether a text is too difficult by reading a 100-word passage and putting down one finger each time the student comes to a word he or she does not know and realizing a text might be too difficult if he or she puts down four fingers and a thumb for unknown words.

running record An individually administered assessment, developed by Clay (1991), using a text for the child to read aloud as the teacher follows a marking system for oral reading, including a system for recording errors (miscues) using Clay's three cueing systems: semantic cues (does it make sense?), syntactic cues (does it sound right?), and visual cues (does it look right?).

scanning A quick form of rapid processing of text, searching for specific details or information.

semantic cues The means used to unlock unknown words based on the reader's knowledge or sense of meanings of other words and inferences in the surrounding text or the clues to comprehension that assist readers in making meaning based on other words and inferences in the surrounding text.

short vowel sounds The vowel sounds generally found in closed syllables (syllables ending with a consonant), in which the sounds are heard at the beginning of the words, such as *an, egg, is, on, us.*

sight words Words that are immediately recognized and do not require word analysis for identification; usually taught because the words are phonemically irregular or are of extremely high frequency.

sight vocabulary The body of words that a reader knows instantly, the size of which is always increasing.

skimming A quick form of rapid processing of text in which less important information is skipped.

standardized or formal assessment A published test or means of gathering information about learners, with a specified set of instructions and procedures that must be followed and cannot be modified to allow comparisons with other test takers.

structural analysis The means by which words can be recognized by their word parts or meaning units, using roots (base or main parts of words), prefixes (word beginnings placed before roots of words), and suffixes (word endings placed behind roots of words).

suffixes Word parts at the end of a root or word.

syllables Units of sound in which each unit has one vowel sound—is a sound with air being pushed through open lips and identified as being open or closed.

syntactic cues The clues that aid in unlocking unknown words based on the reader's knowledge of the rules and the patterns of language.

substrata theory A hypothesis suggested by Holmes (1965) that comprehension and vocabulary ability are so interconnected that to separate the two is a false notion.

syntax The study of the grammar of language; that is, the rules by which sentences are formed and ordered.

teachable moment An unanticipated or unplanned opportunity that arises during a school day that can lead to real and long-term learning.

think-alouds A sharing technique in which a teacher verbalizes aloud the thought processes taking place, to model how skilled readers read silently to themselves.

vocabulary Those words known and understood by a person, sometimes divided into those known in a learner's listening, speaking, reading and writing vocabularies.

vowel Speech sounds made without stopping the flow of air, as in /a/, /e/, /i/, /o/, and /u/ and sometimes w and y, or the letters representing such speech sounds.

vowel digraphs Two vowels that work together to form one sound, as the /oa/ in loaf or the /ea/ in beat.

word banks Collections of words that students keep, which can be written on note cards and kept in a file box or can be compiled in a list and kept in a notebook; useful for a variety of writing and skill building activities.

word families Groups of words that are similar in pattern, usually referring to sets of rhyming words with the rime at the end of the word, which sound alike and are spelled the same, plus the onset at the beginning of the word.

word recognition The process of being able to determine accurately what a word is in printed form, whether sounding it out, using word structure, syllables, context, or other means.

word sorts A word activity in which students are asked to sort or group words either on individual cards or on a word list, either in a manner prescribed by the teacher (a closed sort) or in categories that make sense to the student or students (an open sort).

word walls Lists of words on large pieces of paper or individually on slips of paper, organized in different ways (sometimes alphabetically, or by topics such as seasons) and affixed to classroom walls.

zone of proximal development (ZPD) The area between the level at which a child is able to work independently and that which the child is able to achieve with help from others, as theorized by Vygotsky (1978).

Author & Title
INDEX

Subject INDEX